DEAR AND HONOURED LADY

BY SIR CHARLES TENNYSON
Shorter Poems of Frederick Tennyson
The Devil and the Lady by Alfred Lord Tennyson
Unpublished Early Poems by Alfred Tennyson

Alfred Tennyson
Six Tennyson Essays

DEAR AND HONOURED LADY

THE CORRESPONDENCE BETWEEN
QUEEN VICTORIA AND
ALFRED TENNYSON

EDITED BY
HOPE DYSON
AND
CHARLES TENNYSON

RUTHERFORD • MADISON • TEANECK
FAIRLEIGH DICKINSON UNIVERSITY PRESS

DEAR AND HONOURED LADY.
©Hope Dyson and Charles Tennyson 1969.
First American edition published 1971
by Associated University Presses, Inc.,
Cranbury, New Jersey 08512

Library of Congress Catalogue Card Number: 72-151284

ISBN: 0-8386-7922-6

Printed in the United States of America

CONTENTS

ILLUSTRATIONS

INTRODUCTION

O<small>N</small> pp. 433–457 of vol. II of his *Tennyson: A Memoir*[1]
Hallam Lord Tennyson printed excerpts from the correspondence which had passed between his father and
Queen Victoria. For reasons of political discretion, however,
many whole letters and passages from others were omitted.
Now, more than sixty-five years after the death of the Queen,
the same considerations do not apply, and it is possible to
publish the correspondence in full, so far as it survives, with
relevant correspondence between the poet and other members
of the Royal family, thus giving a much more complete picture
of the remarkable friendship which developed between the
Queen and her Poet Laureate, two of the most extraordinary
personalities of an extraordinary age.

Queen Victoria's letters are in her characteristic handwriting
and flowing emphatic style, with many underlinings and
practically no corrections, becoming blacker, thicker and less
legible in her old age. We have reproduced the underlinings by
italics.

Practically all the Queen's letters to Tennyson and his son
are preserved, through the generosity of the present Lord
Tennyson, in the Tennyson Research Centre at the City
Library at Lincoln. Some of Tennyson's letters are in the Royal
Archives at Windsor Castle, some only exist in drafts or copies
at the Research Centre. In such cases it is of course not possible
to be sure that we have the actual terms of the letter sent by
the writer. We have therefore indicated where only copies or
drafts are available, using initials to show in whose hand-

[1] Macmillan, London, 1897.

writing these are – e.g. A.T. for the poet, E.T. for his wife Emily Tennyson, and H.T. for his son Hallam. Where alternative drafts have been found we have printed them or explained our reasons for not doing so. We have also printed relevant passages from Queen Victoria's diary and from Emily Lady Tennyson's diary. Unfortunately neither of these is the complete original. The Queen's original diary was destroyed after her death, when a copy was made by Princess Beatrice. This was not an exact copy. Emily Tennyson herself destroyed her original diary, making a summary in her own hand. This is now at Lincoln.

We have not thought it necessary to indicate which letters or parts of letters were omitted from Hallam Lord Tennyson's *Memoir*. This would have seriously encumbered the text and any reader who so desires can easily make the comparison for himself.

We are deeply indebted to Her Majesty the Queen for her gracious permission to publish the letters from Queen Victoria and other members of the Royal family or of the Royal households in this collection, and extracts from Queen Victoria's diary. The letter from the Duke of Argyll to Hallam Lord Tennyson in the Appendix is printed by kind permission of the Librarian of the National Library of Australia at Canberra. We also wish to record our sincere thanks to the Librarian at Windsor Castle and the staff of the Royal Library and of the Royal Archives for the great help which they have given us in our work, also to the Librarian and his staff at the City Library, Lincoln, for their help in dealing with the multifarious material in the Tennyson Research Centre. We owe sincere thanks to Mr Christopher Ricks for calling our attention to the two unpublished early poems, 'The Queen of the Isles' and 'Harp, Harp'. These appear in his comprehensive *The Poems of Tennyson* published by Messrs Longmans in February of this year. Our debt to Lady Longford's brilliant and exhaustive life of Queen Victoria must be generally apparent.

H. D.
C. T.

CHAPTER ONE

THE YOUNG TENNYSON

WHEN Alfred Tennyson reached his fortieth birthday
on August 6th, 1849, no one would have believed that
he would, within fifteen months, be appointed Queen
Victoria's Poet Laureate and would for a generation be the
leading literary figure in the English-speaking world, universally
accepted as the representative poet of the great Victorian Age.

True, he had from earliest boyhood (probably in his tenth or
eleventh year) made up his mind that he would be a poet and
nothing else, and if possible a great poet, but the thirty years
which had elapsed since then did not seem to have brought him
much nearer to his goal.

From the beginning the odds seemed heavily against him. He
had been born in 1809, third of the eleven children[1] of the Rector
of Somersby and Bag Enderby, adjacent parishes in a remote
corner of agricultural Lincolnshire with a total population of
less than a hundred souls. This had continued to be his home
until his twenty-eighth year.

It is hard to realise today what such a life was like.

The Rectory was seven miles from the nearest market town,
Spilsby, which today has a population of less than two thousand
and probably had not much more one hundred and sixty years
ago. Not even the main roads had been macadamised at that
time, and the by-lanes must have been nearly impassable in
winter. The children had no bicycles or ponies and cannot often
have got a ride in the Rector's trap. There was no radio,
no television, no cinema, no theatre within reach. A wandering

---

[1] It is sometimes said that Alfred was the fourth of twelve. The reason is
that the Rector's first child, a boy christened George, died in infancy.

fair in summer time was probably the only sort of public enter-
tainment which ever came their way. When the Rector was in
funds he might have taken a weekly newspaper. But there
were no children's newspapers, no available lending library, and
very few children's books were published. There were no
organised games and the children were confined to such amuse-
ments as they could make for themselves. Fortunately for them
– though not perhaps for their parents – the eleven little
Tennysons all came into existence within a period of twelve-
and-a-quarter years, so they were able to create their own
world – and a strange world it was. They grew up tall, shaggy,
untidy, swarthy and aquiline, more like Spaniards or Romanies
than children of an English Rectory, Frederick, the eldest,
being the only one with the traditional Saxon colouring; and
they were as strange in character as in appearance. Shy, sensitive and imaginative, they roamed the countryside, springing
the traps set by the gamekeepers, fishing in the brooks,
playing romantic games of chivalry (for they were essentially
children of the Gothic Revival) or merely lounging along the
lanes with their noses in books. At home they all, boys and
girls, read and wrote enthusiastically. A popular type of com-
position was a serial to which each child contributed in turn,
putting his instalment under the vegetable dish to be read
aloud after dinner. A serial, devised by Alfred and called *The
Old Horse*, is said to have lasted several weeks, and his ghost
stories were thrillingly popular.

Somersby lies in a wooded valley of the Wolds, a double
range of hills reaching here and there to a height of 500 feet,
one line running north and south between the village and the
sea and the other stretching north-westward towards Market
Rasen and Caistor. The old Rectory stands where these two
ranges join, in a delightful valley, down which runs the brook,
destined to become a familiar element in so many Tennysonian
landscapes. The hillsides are dotted with copses and fine trees
and the valleys hide small villages and hamlets each with its
square-towered church, generally still unspoiled by restoration.
Between the villages are scattered old farmhouses of white

plaster or red brick and an occasional sixteenth- or seventeenth-century manor house. To the east of this range of hills stretches the Marsh, a flat strip of rich reclaimed land intersected with reedy ditches. Beyond this is the North Sea coast, noted for the long rise and fall of the tide over the flat sandy shore and for the long barrier of sand dunes which runs between the shore and the marsh. Here Alfred particularly loved to wander, feeling as though he were standing 'on the spine bone of the world'. At the southern end of the Wolds lies Spilsby and beyond it the famous Lincoln fen which stretches away past Boston Stump to the Wash and the northern boundary of Norfolk.

The young Tennysons owed their education mostly to their father, whose influence on his children for both good and ill was incalculable. Alfred, it is true, was sent for four years, between the ages of seven and eleven, to the Grammar School at Louth, twelve miles to the north. There he was bitterly miserable and said that he learned absolutely nothing. It was to his father, Dr Tennyson (as he was always called after taking the degree of LL.D. at Cambridge in 1813), and his own explorations of his father's remarkable library that Alfred owed his education. There he could find books in Latin, Greek, Hebrew, Syriac, Italian, German and Spanish, and a range of subjects extending from poetry ancient and modern to natural science and metaphysics.[1]

His early poems shew that he studied his father's library intensively and creatively and with extraordinary precocity. The rhythm of words appealed to him almost as soon as he could speak. At five years old, he would stretch out his arms to the breeze and run down the sloping lawn behind the Rectory crying out 'I hear a voice that's calling in the wind'. At seven he 'commenced author', filling a slate one Sunday morning, when he was kept at home by a cold, with blank verse in imitation of Thomson's *The Seasons*. A few years ago there was sold at auction a notebook in which the child had copied his Latin and Greek verses. The label of the book reads

[1] The relics – about half – of this library are now at the Tennyson Research Centre in the City Library at Lincoln.

'Tennyson's Works', showing that at eleven years old he was already looking forward to a career as a poet with a shelf full of publications to his credit. Before his fifteenth birthday he had written at least two verse dramas in the Elizabethan manner, an epic in the style of Sir Walter Scott, several poems in the rhyming couplets of Pope. a long poem in Miltonic blank verse on the tremendous theme of 'Armageddon', the last great battle between the forces of good and evil, and innumerable lyrics. All these poems, though imitative and immature, have a wonderful vitality and zest and are naïvely full of undigested learning. Dr Tennyson, himself a poet and a man of varied interests and talents, was deeply impressed with his son's gifts and helped him with criticism and encouragement, binding with his own hands the notebooks into which the child copied his poems.

Unfortunately Dr Tennyson had a double dose of what Alfred used later to describe as 'the black-bloodedness of the Tennysons'. Outwardly also he was black like his sons – a tall, swarthy, strongly built, quick-striding man with a deep vibrant voice. Fonder of society than his children, and a great taker of snuff, even in the pulpit, the geniality and force of his conversation made him a welcome guest in the genteel houses in and about Spilsby and Horncastle. He was widely read, with an exceptional knowledge of the visual arts, a good musician, playing excellently on the harp, and he wrote effective verse in a Byronic vein, though he never published. Taking a lively interest in the political and social questions of the day, he was neither saint nor mystic, and a casual acquaintance would be likely to put him down as an exceptionally good country parson of the Hanoverian breed.

Unfortunately there were weaknesses which a casual acquaintance was not likely to detect.

Dr Tennyson was the eldest son of George Tennyson, of Bayons Manor, Tealby, in the northern part of the county, a successful lawyer, who, by judicious purchases of land during the American and Napoleonic wars, had raised himself to a position in which he could contemplate elevating the hitherto undistinguished Tennysons to the position of a county family. George Tennyson had, for reasons which have never been fully explained, early formed an unfavourable opinion of his elder son – perhaps he thought (possibly with justice) that the boy was not likely to be capable of leading the family to the exalted position which he coveted for it. At any rate he seems, when young George was still little more than a boy, to have decided to make his second son, Charles, future head of the family and owner of Bayons Manor and the considerable estates associated with it. George he more or less compelled to go into the Church, for which he felt no vocation, and, according to the pluralist practice of the time, secured him as many livings as he thought necessary to keep him and his family in comfort – including (in 1815) the incumbency of Great Grimsby.

Dr Tennyson deeply resented this treatment and it is surely a sign of some inherent weakness in his character that he accepted it, and did not even move from Somersby, when his father procured him the much more important living at Grimsby, where the family had been well known for two or three generations, and his grandfather had, by marriage, acquired a large amount of the land on which the town now stands.

The rapid growth of his family incrèased Dr Tennyson's resentment. Life at the Rectory became more and more difficult. It was quite a small house and sometimes there were as many as twenty-three people living in it, some sleeping five and six in a room. Moreover, Dr Tennyson exhausted himself by taking on the education of his seven sons himself, seeking to find compensation in their success for the frustration and waste of his own abilities. 'Phoenix-like', he wrote, 'I trust (though I don't think myself a Phoenix) they will spring from my ashes in consequence of the exertions I have bestowed on them'.

The result was disastrous. Dr Tennyson's health, both mental and physical, rapidly deteriorated. Before long he sought relief in drink, causing distressing scenes of violence at the Rectory and much gossip and scandal in the neighbourhood.

The children inevitably suffered much, both directly and

from an agonising sense of divided loyalties. They were genuinely devoted both to their father and to their mother, a woman of simple piety and so tender-hearted that the village boys of Somersby used to beat their dogs under the Rectory windows, knowing that she would immediately run out and offer them money to desist. The seven sons were particularly hard hit. Frederick, the eldest, who was to inherit the Grimsby property, escaped to Italy as soon as he could and only returned to England to die more than sixty years later. Charles, the second son, and Alfred's favourite brother, became an opium addict and only recovered, after many years of struggle, through the devoted help of his wife, who suffered a serious and prolonged mental breakdown as the result of her exertions. Of the three next below Alfred in age, the life of one was wrecked by drink for nearly thirty years, one spent the last sixty years of his existence in an asylum, the third one, a man of brilliant gifts, died a nervous wreck in his fifty-second year. Only the seventh, Horatio, who was ten years younger than Alfred and born too late to feel the full effect of the worst years of crisis, escaped to drift not unhappily, though rather aimlessly, through life, always seeming, as Edward FitzGerald once described him, 'rather unused to the planet'.

On Alfred, who passed through the worst of the crisis during the acutely sensitive years of his adolescence, the impact was severe. Often, when he could endure the tension at home no longer, he would run across the narrow lane which separates the Rectory from the churchyard and fling himself down among the tombstones, longing for death.

To such experiences as these he owed the morbid shyness, the horror of gossip, the extreme sensibility to criticism and the frequent bouts of depression which were to afflict him throughout his long life.

He was saved from immediate disaster by the generosity of an aunt, which made it possible for him to go to Trinity College, Cambridge, in the autumn of 1827.

Until that time he had hardly ever been more than 30 miles from Somersby, and his shyness and rusticity made the sudden plunge into the noisy inquisitive student life of the university painful to him, but his striking appearance and the imaginative force of his conversation soon made their mark.

At the end of 1828 or early in 1829 there occurred what was to be the most fateful event of his life. He met and quickly formed a passionately intimate friendship with Arthur Hallam.

No two men could well have been more different in personality and circumstance, for Arthur was a son of Henry Hallam, the historian, one of the leading literary men of the day and a highly respected figure in London Society. Arthur had been sent to Eton, where he had been regarded as the leading debater and poet in the school and universally beloved for his brilliant and unselfish charm. From Eton he came in due course to Trinity with the whole university open to him for a choice of friends. At Eton his closest friend had been W. E. Gladstone. At Cambridge his choice fell on Alfred Tennyson.

The stimulus and support of this friendship was of incalculable value to Tennyson, giving him new confidence and helping him to combat the depressive tendencies with which the miseries of life at Somersby had afflicted him. In the spring of 1829 the friends were both elected members of 'The Apostles', a secret society of University intellectuals which had been founded a few years before and which still exists. A month later Tennyson was adjudged winner of the Chancellor's Gold Medal for English Verse. In June 1830 he published his first volume, *Poems Chiefly Lyrical*, which, though it contained a few lyrics of the highest quality, made little impact on the public. At the end of the year Arthur's engagement to Tennyson's sister Emily, drew the friends still closer together.

In January 1831 Dr Tennyson died, a broken and despondent wreck of fifty-one, and Alfred had to leave Cambridge without a degree in order to look after the family. But the friendship remained as close as ever. Urged on by Arthur, he brought out his second volume at the end of 1832. This, though it contained (admittedly in less perfect form than we know them today) some of his most famous poems, such as 'Oenone', 'The Lady of

Shalott' and 'The Lotos-Eaters', was savagely attacked by
leading critics, with disastrous effect on its sales and on the
poet's reputation. But for his friend's support, the effect on the
poet himself might have been equally disastrous.

Then in October of 1833 Arthur Hallam died suddenly in
Vienna while on a holiday tour with his father.

The blow to Tennyson was crushing and for some months he
almost lost the will to live. But he rallied and spent the next
four years in seclusion at Somersby, devoting himself chiefly to
the revision of his already published poems, and to an intensive
study of Natural Science and Philosophy by which he hoped to
equip himself for more serious work in the future.

In 1837 the family had to leave Somersby, as the Rectory was
needed by a new incumbent. It is probable that by this time
Tennyson had completed very little work not actually begun
before Arthur's death except 'Ulysses' and some of the earlier
sections of *In Memoriam*, out of which he had as yet no idea of
making a complete poem. His feelings on leaving Somersby are
chronicled in the clearly contemporary sections c–ciii of *In
Memoriam*. In spite of the suffering and disasters of those early
years, they had brought him unforgettable delights, first in the
budding affections and sensibilities of childhood and adolescence, and later in the intense spiritual communion with his
friend. Forgetting now his early miseries he felt these memories

> *. . . mix in one another's arms*
> *To one pure image of regret.*

But there was another feeling, recorded in the dream which he
describes in Section ciii. He seemed to be gliding out of the
quiet stream of his early restricted life, past its level meads and
banks shadowed by

> *. . . iris, and the golden reed . . .*

into a grander flood with vaster shores, until at last, where the
forward-creeping tides began to break in foam, a great ship
lifted her shining sides. On the deck was Arthur, now a giant

form 'thrice as large as man'

> *And while the wind began to sweep*
> *A music out of sheet and shroud,*

The two friends steered the great ship

> *. . . toward a crimson cloud*
> *That landlike slept along the deep.*

CHAPTER TWO

'OUT OF THE BURROW'

THE Tennysons now moved to an old house at High Beech in Epping Forest, apparently attracted to the place by the residence, at what is now Arabin House, Loughton, of an eminent lawyer, Sergeant Arabin, whose wife was a friend, perhaps a relative, of Alfred's mother.

They arrived within a few months of the accession of Queen Victoria on June 20th, 1837.

The reign of the little Queen had begun with extraordinary *éclat*. Born just ten years later than Tennyson, she had lost her father before her first birthday and had been brought up by her German mother, the Duchess of Kent, and German governess in dull, but not inactive, seclusion, until the impending death of the childless King George the Fourth, and the accession of his childless brother William, made it reasonably certain that she would become Queen. Immediately her small person became the centre of a vortex of Court intrigue, unfortunate results of which were her complete alienation from her mother who nevertheless kept her under the most rigid control, and her excessive submission to the influence of her sympathetic but not very discreet German governess Lehzen. For neither of these misfortunes could the young Princess be held responsible. Indeed few girls could have survived without serious psychological damage the almost unrelieved atmosphere of jealousy, gossip and spite, in which the most sensitive years of Victoria's adolescence were passed, or maintained her independence and sincerity after being so long and so unscrupulously manipulated by rival factions for their own interests.

During her early childhood she had owed much to her

mother's brother Leopold, who had been the husband for two years of the tragic Princess Charlotte, George IV's daughter. Leopold, astute, statesmanlike, affectionate, had called at Kensington Palace every week, and Victoria had paid him almost weekly visits at Claremont near Esher, the house which Parliament had given him on the death of his wife. But in 1830, the year in which the death of George IV brought in the most difficult period of Victoria's childhood, Leopold left England to become King of the Belgians.

She grew up intelligent, extraordinarily honest, highly emotional, impulsive and hot tempered, with great vitality and a keen power of enjoyment. She was not intellectual, but she had a good knowledge of history, in which she was keenly interested, spoke French and German fluently and had some knowledge of Italian, chiefly acquired at the opera which she adored. She had a good ear for music and a pleasant clear voice (her speaking voice was extraordinarily clear, firm and melodious), and she danced with remarkable skill and enthusiasm. Literature did not mean much to her, though she took pleasure in Sir Walter Scott's poetry. Above all she was courageous and independent, and, although under five feet in height, had an extraordinary natural dignity which she maintained even when she had lost her blue-eyed, flaxen-haired, round-cheeked girlish charm, and become hook-nosed and dumpy. Her walk, which had an almost martial decision, increased the tiny figure's remarkable impact.

Immediately after William IV's death secured her position, Victoria seized with extraordinary courage and independence the advantages which it offered her. Her Ministers and Councillors were astonished at the ease, self-possession and good sense with which she carried out her duties. The public were carried away with enthusiasm. 'What, above all, struck everybody with overwhelming force', wrote Lytton Strachey, 'was the contrast between Queen Victoria and her Uncles. The nasty old men, debauched and selfish, pig-headed and ridiculous, with their perpetual burden of debts, confusions, and disreputabilities – they had vanished like the snows of winter, and here at last, crowned and radiant, was the spring'.

It is clear that Alfred Tennyson's spirits reacted strongly to the promise of the new reign. Scandal about the Court must have reached him even in the days of his boyhood at Somersby for his precocious drama *The Devil and the Lady*, written in or before his fifteenth year, contains slighting references to Almack's and Lady Jersey (George IV's mistress), and there exist amongst Dr Tennyson's papers some pungent verses addressed to George III (presumably by the Doctor himself) which shew that the Rector held strong views about the relations of the Prince of Wales (afterwards King George IV) with his wife, Princess Caroline of Brunswick, and their daughter Princess Charlotte. Here are a few relevant stanzas.

24

What tho' giddy sons perplex thee,
Shake their elbows, drink and wh–,
What tho' wanton Jersey vex thee,
Veteran Fitzherbert more?

25

What tho' of his wife and daughter
England's hope forgetful prove,
And by base contrivance sought her
Life, who ought to be his love?

26

What tho' Brunswick's Issue ducal
Be neglected and reviled,
And thy son to make us puke all
Wish't to bastardise his child?

27

What tho' still the jaundiced Charlotte
Stimulate her impious son
Yet to stigmatise as harlot
One as spotless as the sun?

28

What tho' he in tricks detected
From Newmarket was kicked off,

And unworthily rejected
Even of fools and knaves the scoff? . . .

No doubt young Alfred had shared these views. Now he dashed off some light-hearted stanzas ('little more than newspaper verse' he called them) which he sent to his friend James Spedding in the hope that Spedding might be able to get them printed in *The Times*. Tennyson's reputation was, however, just then at about its lowest point and the verses failed to appear, nor were they ever published in his lifetime, though Hallam Lord Tennyson printed the fifth stanza in his *Memoir* of his father (vol. I, p. 161). They now appear in *The Poems of Tennyson*, ed. Christopher Ricks.

'THE QUEEN OF THE ISLES'

My friends since you wish for a health from the host,
Come fill up your glasses: I'll give you a toast.
Let us drink to the health that we value the most –
To the health of the Queen of the Isles.

The reigns of her fathers were long or were short,
They plagued us in anger or vext us in sport.
Let them sleep in their good or their evil report –
But a health to the Queen of the Isles.

May those in her council that have the chief voice
Be true hearts of oak that the land may rejoice
And the people may love her the more for her choice –
So a health to the Queen of the Isles.

No slaves of a party, straightforward and clear,
Let them speak out like men without bias or fear
That the voice of her people may reach to her ear
With a health to the Queen of the Isles.

That the voice of a satisfied people may keep
A sound in her ear like the sound of the deep,
Like the voice of the sea when the wind is asleep
And a health to the Queen of the Isles.

Let her flag as (of old) be the first on the seas,
That the good of the land and the world may increase

And Power may balance the nations in Peace
  With a health to the Queen of the Isles.

But if despots and fools must be taught with the rod,
Let her soldier tread firm as his fathers have trod,
And her cannon roar out like the judgement of God
  With a health to the Queen of the Isles.

My brothers and friends! may the days that commence
Be so fruitful in genius, in worth and in sense
That a man's eye shall glisten, a thousand years hence,
  When he reads of the Queen of the Isles!

And since Time never pauses but Change must ensue,
Let us wish that old things may fit well with the new,
For the blessing of promise is on her like dew –
  So a health to the Queen of the Isles.

God bless her! and long may she hold the command
Till the hair of the boy shall be gray in the land
And the ball and the sceptre shall pass from her hand
  To the race of the Queen of the Isles.

So fill up your glasses and hold them on high,
Were the health fathoms-deep I would drink it or die,
And send out your voices and join in the cry
  To the health of the Queen of the Isles.

And there were other causes for Tennyson's new optimism.
The move to Epping Forest had given him the opportunity to
renew relations with old friends and to make new ones. People
had not yet grown disillusioned about the hopes excited by the
passage of the Reform Act of 1832, the abolition of slavery and
Catholic Emancipation. The rapid development of the railways
and other scientific and industrial advances seemed to offer
the prospect of unprecedented material and spiritual development. 'Locksley Hall', written about this time, gave antiphonal
expression to the hopes and the half-realised apprehensions of
the age. It was no doubt a further sign of Tennyson's newly
found optimism that in 1838 he became engaged to Emily
Sellwood, who was to become his wife twelve years later. In
1840 the Sellwoods broke off the engagement, on the grounds
that Tennyson, who still refused to publish, shewed no sign of

being able to earn a living for a wife and family. Probably there was also some disapproval of the breadth of his religious opinions and his bohemian way of life, which included the smoking of much strong tobacco in a short clay pipe and the nightly consumption of a pint of port when he could afford it – and probably often when he could not.

In 1842 he published two volumes (one of revised, one of new work) partly no doubt in the hope of advancing his cause with the Sellwoods, but mainly because of a threat from New England, where his two early volumes had become very popular, that these would be reissued in America in their unrevised form unless he republished them himself.

The new volumes met with a much better critical reception than that of 1832, and sold fairly well. Then in 1843 came a crushing blow. Tennyson lost the whole of his small capital, probably about two thousand pounds, through a rash investment, made no doubt in the hope of re-establishing his position with the Sellwoods.

The shock to the highly sensitive poet's health, both mental and bodily, was so severe that his friends began to fear for his reason, and even for his life.

Now, however, there were several people of eminence among his friends, and these in 1845 persuaded Sir Robert Peel, the Prime Minister of the day, that Tennyson was a poet of merit who could never hope to earn a living by his verse. Peel therefore granted him a pension of two hundred pounds a year from the Civil List.

This gave Tennyson new hope. He now completed *The Princess*, the poem on the position and rights of women, on which he had been working for several years. This was published in 1847 and, after a discouraging start, soon began to gain popular favour.

But Peel's grant sparked off an even more important development – perhaps the most important in Tennyson's entire life. Beginning immediately after Arthur Hallam's death in 1833, he had been jotting down in a simple stanza form, wherever he might be and just as the thought occurred to him, short lyrics expressive of his emotions and reflexions arising from the loss of his friend. He had done this intermittently in odd notebooks, often on old scraps of paper, without any thought of continuity or ultimate publication.

Soon after the publication of the 1842 volumes he seems to have assembled these poems and fragments and realised for the first time that they might be given some degree of continuity and logical form. *The Princess* out of the way, his thoughts turned again to his 'Elegies' as he called them, but he still could not make up his mind to publish. He always disliked the idea of publication as an exposure to misunderstanding and possibly stupid attack of his intimate thoughts and emotions, and these 'Elegies' had to him an almost sacred character. Now, however, there was a strong incentive to overcome his reluctance. With the moderate success of *The Princess*, the chances of a new approach to the Sellwoods seemed more propitious. He consulted his publisher, Edward Moxon, who was optimistic and offered an advance on royalties of £500. Tennyson sent a copy of the manuscript to Emily. She reacted enthusiastically – incidentally suggesting the title, *In Memoriam*, under which the poem has become the most famous of the great Victorian Age. Even then Alfred seems to have wavered and hesitated. Long years of failure and frustration had sapped his morale and impaired his power to make a decision which would change his whole way of life and perhaps expose him to malignancy and misunderstanding. But at last he took the plunge. On June 1st, 1850 the poem was published. On June 13th Alfred and Emily were married. It is characteristic of Tennyson's extreme shyness and sensibility and his shrinking from publicity that he told none of his friends or relations, not even his beloved mother, of his decision to marry.

In Memoriam was an immediate and resounding success, even more with the general reader than with the critics, though these too soon joined in the chorus of acclaim.

Amongst the most fervent admirers of the poem was Prince Albert.

Largely through his influence Tennyson was in November of

this, his *annus mirabilis*, 1850, offered the Poet Laureateship in succession to Wordsworth, who had died on April 23rd.

He had had no thought that the post might be offered him, or even that his claim was being canvassed. It was therefore a remarkable coincidence that on the night before he received the letter from Windsor Castle he should have dreamed that the Prince came and kissed him on the cheek and that he commented in his dream 'very kind, but very German'.

CHAPTER THREE

POET LAUREATE

THERE is no evidence that Queen Victoria took any special interest in the appointment of her Poet Laureate. She had little knowledge of contemporary literature and it is unlikely that she had read Tennyson's volumes of 1842 or *The Princess*. Moreover these mid-century years were the fullest and most domestically absorbing of her married life. She had been married to Albert for just over ten years, during which she had gradually devolved on him more and more of her official duties. She still loved him with unabated intensity and, in spite of her dislike of the process of child-bearing ('the shadow side of marriage' she called it), had already borne him six children, the sixth (Prince Arthur) making its appearance in May 1850 and no doubt occupying most of her activity and attention during the last half of this crucial year. At first there had been some jealousy of Albert's extreme competence and wide knowledge, for he had already served a very strict political apprenticeship under the supervision of King Leopold and Baron Stockmar, a man known and respected in all the courts of Europe, but before their marriage was two years old she had arranged for him to have copies of all official papers and he prepared all political business for her and drafted all important letters for her consideration. In fact he soon became King in all but name and, although of course he could not attend meetings of the cabinet, an informal and highly influential member of all governments. Albert had come into her life when the disastrous Flora Hastings scandal and her unfortunate clash with Sir Robert Peel had brought to an end the ecstatic first phase of her reign. Since then he had reconciled her to her mother,

reorganised the Royal Household, and restored the finances of
the Duchy of Cornwall and the Windsor Estates, thus freeing the
monarchy from the perpetual bickering with Parliament over
finance which had been so prejudicial to it in the past. He had
also acquired the estates at Osborne and Balmoral where the
Queen spent more and more time as the years passed. He loved
country life and had taught her to love it, for he was a fine
horseman, an excellent shot and a beautiful skater. His rather
stiff military figure and regular – if rather expressionless –
features had a teutonic beauty. He was a devoted and infinitely
considerate husband and father. Though stiff and formal in
society, he had, in family life, an engaging teutonic playfulness.
He shared her love of music and dancing. It was small wonder
that his young wife (she was still only thirty years old) adored
him and left more and more responsibility in his hands.

This tendency and Tennyson's shyness and diffidence were
no doubt the reasons why no personal relation developed between the Queen and her Laureate during the 1850s.

Indeed Tennyson had plenty during these years to absorb
his energies. For him there now began a new life, or perhaps
two new lives – a private and a public one.

Emily was to make him an ideal mate. Combining real charm
and intelligence with an iron will and a strong sense of duty,
she devoted her whole energy to securing his health, and, so far
as she could, his happiness, and providing him with the best
possible conditions in which to do his work. Herself she kept
entirely in the background.

'The peace of God came into my life when I married her', he
said to a friend whom he met when he returned from his honey-
moon, and thirty-five years later, in the second 'Locksley Hall',
he included two lines which undoubtedly expressed his feelings
about what she had done for him.

Very woman of very woman, nurse of ailing body and mind,
She that linked again the broken chain that bound me to my kind.

A closer link with his fellow-men was also an inevitable result
of his new position as Laureate. On March 6th, 1851, he

attended a levee at Buckingham Palace. He had missed the first levee of the new year because he hadn't been able to borrow a Court suit and he couldn't afford to buy one. Then a friend, Samuel Rogers, the old Banker poet, offered to lend his. This had been worn by Wordsworth at his presentation in 1843 and Rogers had promised to leave it to the Wordsworth family. Rogers was a small man and the suit was a tight fit, but Alfred was delighted with the cocked hat and with the appearance of his magnificent legs in black silk stockings. Thackeray, on whom he called one day, found him as pleased and innocent as a child about the whole affair.

His attendance at the levee on March 6th, does not seem to have led to any personal contact with the Queen or Prince Albert, although no doubt he was formally 'presented'. However, a few days later, at a party at the house of the Prime Minister, Lord John Russell, he made a new friend who was to be of the greatest importance to him in his relations with the Court, George Campbell, 8th Duke of Argyll, statesman, scientist, poet and son-in-law of the Duchess of Sutherland, who had been Queen Victoria's Mistress of the Robes since her accession and had become the most beloved and trusted of all her ladies.

The Duke was the most courteous of men and a fervent admirer of Tennyson's poetry. He now spoke warmly of his pleasure on at last having the opportunity to make the poet's acquaintance. 'You won't find much in me after all', was Tennyson's unexpected reply.

From the first the new Laureate took his official position seriously. He had long been interested in the generalities of social and political development. His interest now began to embrace the practical problems of the hour. His first Laureate poem was the dedication 'To the Queen' of the Seventh Edition of his two volumes of 1842, which was issued in April, 1851. The poem is dated 'March 1851' and was therefore probably written after his first personal contact with the Queen at the levee of March 6th. It reproduced, in more ceremonial language, the general tone of the verses to 'The Queen of the Isles', and has been reprinted, in a slightly revised form, as the dedication in all Editions of his Collected Works. We print it here in the form in which it first appeared.[1]

No record survives of the Queen's reaction to this poem, but she must surely have found it congenial, although no doubt her interpretation of the Royal function would have included some more positive claim to initiative on the part of the Sovereign.

'TO THE QUEEN'

Revered Victoria, you that hold
A nobler office upon earth
Than arms, or power of brain, or birth
Could give the warrior kings of old,

I thank you that your Royal grace
To one of less desert allows
This laurel greener from the brows
Of him that utter'd nothing base:

And should your greatness, and the care
That yokes with empire, yield you time
To make demands of modern rhyme
If aught of ancient worth be there,

[1] The chief differences between the original and final versions of the poem are the omission from the later versions of the stanza referring to the Great Exhibition, perhaps because Tennyson came to realise that the Prince Consort and not the Queen had been the true originator of the Exhibition scheme, (this stanza was in fact omitted from the 8th edition issued in 1852) and the inclusion of a charming fourth stanza:

> *Then – while a sweeter music wakes,*
> *And through wild March the throstle calls,*
> *Where all about your palace-walls*
> *The sun-lit almond-blossom shakes –*

Hallam Tennyson in the annotated editions of the *Works* (p. 895) says that there was originally a third stanza (omitted only at the proof-stage) which read as follows:

> *Nor should I dare to flatter State*
> *ˌNor such a lay would you receive*
> *Were I to shape it, who believe*
> *Your nature true as you are great.*

Both inclusion and omission of this stanza are evidence of Tennyson's high opinion of the Queen's character even before he had any personal contact with her.

Take, Madam, this poor book of song;
   For tho' the faults were thick as dust
   In vacant chambers I could trust
Your kindness. May you rule us long,

And leave us rulers of your blood
   As noble till the latest day!
   May children of our children say,
'She wrought her people lasting good:

'Her court was pure; her life serene;
   God gave her peace; her land reposed;
   A thousand claims to reverence closed
In her as Mother, Wife, and Queen;

'She brought a vast design to pass,
   When Europe and the scatter'd ends
   Of our fierce world were mixt as friends
And brethren in her halls of glass;

'And statesmen at her council met
   Who knew the seasons, when to take
   Occasion by the hand, and make
The bounds of freedom broader yet

'By shaping some august decree
   Which kept her throne unshaken still,
   Broad-based upon her people's will,
And compass'd by the inviolate sea.'

March, 1851

1852 saw Tennyson rush, with sudden and what must seem to us today uncharacteristic, violence, into the political arena. Prince Louis Napoleon, who had been elected President of the French Democratic Republic soon after the fall of Louis Philippe in 1848, had ever since been working cautiously and craftily to destroy the party of the left and acquire absolute authority for himself. On December 2nd, 1851, he carried out a *coup d'état*, with what the wife of the British Ambassador called 'dreadful and undiscriminating bloodshed', and had himself proclaimed 'Emperor of the French'. Early in 1852 it became known that he was restoring the Imperial Eagles to the uniforms and flags of the French army. A wave of apprehension swept through Britain.

*Alfred and Emily Tennyson with their sons Hallam (right) and Lionel.
A photograph taken at Farringford by Julia Margaret Cameron in the
early 1860s.*

A rough sketch for the Spy cartoon of Alfred Tennyson

Tennyson caught the infection as did his young friend, the poet Coventry Patmore. Patmore launched a plan for setting up Volunteer Rifle Clubs all over the country. The idea appealed to Tennyson who sent him three stanzas entitled 'Rifle Clubs!!!' for use in his campaign. Though Patmore published a letter advocating his scheme in *The Times* of January 22nd, 1852, Tennyson's exceedingly spirited lines were not published until Mr Christopher Ricks included them in his comprehensive edition of Tennyson's Poems, already referred to.

'RIFLE CLUBS!!!'

Peace is thirty-seven years old,
Sweet Peace can no man blame,
But Peace of sloth or of avarice born,
Her olive is her shame;
And I dreamt of Charon alone in my bed –
His boat was crammed and he rose and said
'I carry the dead, the dead, the dead,
    Killed in the Coup d'Etat'.

Half a million of men in arms,
Yet peace we all require,
Half a million of men in arms,
And the head of them all a liar.
'They wronged him not', the ferryman said,
'Yet look at his bullets in heart and head –
So I carry the dead, the dead, the dead,
    Killed in the Coup d'Etat'

Some love Peace for her own dear sake,
Tradesmen love her for gain,
But in France the rifle is all-in-all,
And the crimson trousers reign –
'Children and women – their wounds are red,
And I wait for Louis', the ferryman said,
'To follow the dead, the dead, the dead,
    Killed in the Coup d'Etat'.

This was by no means the end of Tennyson's burst of political activity. On January 31st, 1852, he published in his friend John Forster's paper, *The Examiner*, a poem of extra-ordinary violence under the title 'Britons, Guard your Own'. The first and last stanzas of this not very distinguished poem will give an idea of its quality.

> *RISE, Britons, rise, if manhood be not dead;*
> *The world's last tempest darkens overhead;*
> *   The Pope has bless'd him;*
> *   The Church caress'd him;*
> *He triumphs; maybe, we shall stand alone:*
> *   Britons, guard your own. . . .*
>
> *Should he land here, and for one hour prevail,*
> *There must no man go back to bear the tale:*
> *   No man to bear it –*
> *   Swear it! We swear it!*
> *Although we fought the banded world alone,*
> *   We swear to guard our own.*

This poem appeared over the signature 'Merlin' because Tennyson, feared that if he used his own name, his views might be taken as official and compromise the Queen and the government who had decided to remain passive on the issue.

On February 7th *The Examiner* published a less violent and more statesman-like poem by Tennyson (also over the signature 'Merlin') called 'The Third of February – 1852'. This poem was occasioned by the action of the House of Lords, who on February 3rd had rejected the Bill for the organisation of the Militia, which had been brought forward because of the crisis. Four stanzas out of the eight will show the poem's tone and quality.

'THE THIRD OF FEBRUARY
1852'

> *My Lords, we heard you speak: you told us all*
> *   That England's honest censure went too far;*
> *That our free press should cease to brawl,*
> *   Not sting the fiery Frenchman into war.*
> *It was our ancient privilege, my Lords,*
> *To fling whate'er we felt, not fearing, into words. . . .*

As long as we remain, we must speak free,
  Tho' all the storm of Europe on us break:
No little German state are we,
  But the one voice in Europe; we must speak;
That if to-night our greatness were struck dead,
There might be left some record of the things we said.

Shall we fear him? our own we never fear'd.
  From our first Charles by force we wrung our claims.
Prick'd by the Papal spur, we rear'd,
  We flung the burthen of the second James.
I say, we never feared! and as for these,
We broke them on the land, we drove them on the seas. . . .

Tho' niggard throats of Manchester may bawl,
  What England was, shall her true sons forget?
We are not cotton-spinners all,
  But some love England and her honour yet.
And these in our Thermopylae shall stand,
And hold against the world this honour of the land.

In the same number *The Examiner* printed yet another
poem by Tennyson (still over the signature 'Merlin'), entitled
'Hands All Round' – Walter Savage Landor, reading this in
The Examiner, called it, perhaps rather extravagantly, 'in-
comparably the best (*convivial*) lyric in the language'. It is of
special interest today for the two concluding stanzas addressed
to the United States.

  Gigantic daughter of the West
    We drink to thee across the flood,
  We know thee most, we love thee best,
    For art thou not of British blood?
  Should war's mad blast again be blown,
    Permit not thou the tyrant powers
  To fight thy mother here alone,
    But let thy broadsides roar with ours.
        Hands all round!
    God the tyrant's cause confound!
  To our great kinsmen of the West, my friends,
    And the great name of England round and round.

> *O rise, our strong Atlantic sons,*
>   *When war against our freedom springs!*
> *O speak to Europe through your guns!*
>   *They can be understood by kings.*
> *You must not mix our Queen with those*
>   *That wish to keep their people fools;*
> *Our freedom's foemen are her foes,*
>   *She comprehends the race she rules.*
>   *Hands all round!*
>   *God the tyrant's cause confound!*
> *To our dear kinsmen of the West, my friends,*
>   *And the great name of England round and round.*

Even this was not the end of Tennyson's remarkable outburst.
In *The Examiner*'s issue of February 14th appeared the most
singular of all the series. It had the title 'Suggested by Reading
an Article in a Newspaper' and was preceded by a letter signed
under a new pseudonym 'Taliessin', in the following terms:

To the Editor of *The Examiner*

SIR, – I have read with much interest the poems of Merlin.
The enclosed is longer than either of those, and certainly not
so good: yet as I flatter myself that it has a smack of Merlin's
style in it, and as I feel that it expresses forcibly enough some of
the feelings of our time, perhaps you may be induced to admit
it.

TALIESSIN

This singular poem (see *Poems of Tennyson*, London:
Longmans, 1969, 1004–7) is addressed to the Press, urging it to
match up to its great responsibilities. The connection with the
coup d'état crisis only appears in the last stanza, but the poem is
of interest as an effective example of a kind of satire in which
Tennyson very rarely indulged. Here are six of the concluding
stanzas:

> *I feel the thousand cankers of our State,*
>   *I fain would shake their triple-folded ease,*
> *The hogs who can believe in nothing great,*
>   *Sneering bedridden in the down of Peace*
> *Over their scrips and shares, their meats and wine,*
> *With stony smirks at all things human and divine!*

I honour much, I say, this man's appeal.
  We drag so deep in our commercial mire,
We move so far from greatness, that I feel
  Exception to be character'd in fire.
Who looks for Godlike greatness here shall see
The British Goddess, sleek Respectability.

Alas for her and all her small delights!
  She feels not how the social frame is rack'd.
She loves a little scandal which excites;
  A little feeling is a want of tact.
For her there lie in wait millions of foes,
And yet the 'not too much' is all the rule she knows.

Poor soul! behold her: what decorous calm!
  She, with her week-day worldliness sufficed,
Stands in her pew and hums her decent psalm
  With decent dippings at the name of Christ!
And she has mov'd in that smooth way so long,
She hardly can believe that she shall suffer wrong. . . .

Alas, our youth, so clever yet so small,
  Thin dilettanti deep in nature's plan,
Who make the emphatic One, by whom is all,
  An essence less concentred than a man!
Better wild Mahmoud's war-cry once again!
O fools, we want a manlike God and Godlike men!

Go, frightful omens. Yet once more I turn
  To you that mould men's thoughts; I call on you
To make opinion warlike, lest we learn
  A sharper lesson than we ever knew.
I hear a thunder though the skies are fair,
But shrill you, loud and long, the warning-note:
  Prepare!

The Great Duke of Wellington died on September 14th.
Tennyson, who remembered the London Coach driving into
Spilsby decorated with white ribands in honour of the Victory
of Waterloo, had a special respect and admiration for the old
victor. Only a few years before he had refused the offer of an
introduction to the Duke at an evening party – 'what should
the great Duke want with a poor poet like me?' Now he set

about what was to prove one of his grandest achievements, unrivalled for sustained emotion, metrical originality, grandeur of melody and imaginative force. Although the fear of a French invasion had waned, Tennyson repeated the warning urged in the previous poems against the lack of military preparation, which has so often landed our country in almost fatal difficulties. Of particular interest for our present purpose is the brief reference to the British Monarchy.

> *O Statesmen, guard us, guard the eye, the soul*
> *Of Europe, keep our noble England whole,*
> *And save the one true seed of freedom sown*
> *Betwixt a people and their ancient throne,*
> *That sober freedom out of which there springs*
> *Our loyal passion for our temperate kings . . .*

A strange reference, for it could hardly be said that the English people had ever shewn much 'passion' for its Hanoverian Kings, or that the epithet 'temperate' was conspicuously appropriate to them. In fact I think Tennyson must have had his mind fixed on a Queen, not a King, and that perhaps he meant to include in his reference that Queen's Consort, Prince Albert, for whom he had by this time conceived a high admiration.

The Queen must have seen the Wellington Ode, though no reference to it has been found in her correspondence or diary. Probably she did not see *The Examiner* poems. If she had she would no doubt have approved them, for she shared Tennyson's and the British people's alarm at Napoleon III's manœuvres and the country's lack of military preparation.

The Queen and her Laureate seem also to have reacted in much the same way to the onset and development of the Crimean War, in which Britain became involved on March 28th, 1854 – surprisingly enough as ally of Napoleon III in defence of the Turks against the Russians. The only evidence of Tennyson's early reaction is in his letter of invitation to his friend (and his elder son's Godfather), the Rev. F. D. Maurice, to visit Farringford, the home which Alfred and

Emily had at last found, after three years of search, at the west end of the Isle of Wight.

> *For groves of pine on either hand,*
> *To break the blast of winter, stand;*
> * And further on, the hoary Channel*
> *Tumbles a billow on chalk and sand;*
>
> *Where, if below the milky steep*
> *Some ship of battle slowly creep,*
> * And on thro' zones of light and shadow*
> *Glimmer away to the lonely deep,*
>
> *We might discuss the Northern sin*
> *Which made a selfish war begin;*
> * Dispute the claims, arrange the chances;*
> *Emperor, Ottoman, which shall win;*
>
> *Or whether war's avenging rod*
> *Shall lash all Europe into blood;*
> * Till you should turn to dearer matters,*
> *Dear to the man that is dear to God;*

The poem was written (the last stanza suggests this) before 'The Wreath of March' had blossomed – therefore, clearly, before the actual declaration of war, and its tone suggests a certain detachment. Indeed it is by no means clear to which side the epithet 'selfish' is applied. The Queen also had been outraged by the *coup d'état* and when this 'unsatisfactory war', as she at first called it, had got under way, she quickly became involved in its *mystique* (the phrase is Lady Longford's), arising, as Mr Hector Bolitho has said, from 'the curious ancient bonds between the army and its monarch'. She now threw herself with enthusiasm into the part of Britain's Queen at War. She watched with emotion from the balcony at Buckingham Palace as her Guards marched by on their way to the front. She waved her pocket-handkerchief from the deck of the Royal Yacht as her Fleet came out from Spithead with all sail set 'giving us three hearty cheers, as I think none but British tars can give'. She stood for hours presenting medals to the soldiers from the battle front – many of them cruelly wounded.

As for the Prince, 'The talent for administration', writes Strachey, 'which had reorganised the Royal Palaces and planned the Great Exhibition asserted itself no less in the confused complexities of war. Again and again the Prince's suggestions, rejected or unheeded at first, were adopted under the stress of circumstances and found to be full of value.'

Tennyson, in his more detached way, also felt the *mystique*. He had always (however vaguely) hankered after the life of action which his extreme short sight denied him. Indeed Edward Fitzgerald thought of him as a man ideally fitted to have captained a Greek warship at the Battle of Salamis. Now after reading in *The Times* a report of the famous but futile charge of the Light Brigade, he dashed off his famous ballad and sent it to the *The Examiner*. Copies of this found their way to the Crimea and the ballad immediately became so popular with the troops that an army chaplain wrote begging him to send copies for distribution amongst them. Here was a request which could not be refused and he had several thousand copies of a special leaflet printed and sent to the front without delay.

At home the poem aroused considerable controversy owing to its unconventional form and off beat rhymes. If the Queen saw it, as she most probably did, she would have approved its spirit and indignantly repudiated the criticisms. But the course of the 'unsatisfactory war' stirred Tennyson to more far-reaching thought, as for example about the differences between private and collective violence; between just and unjust war; between physical violence and the 'civil war' of exploiter against exploited – 'The viler as underhand, not openly bearing the sword', between war as a cause and a consequence and, finally, of war as the supreme sacrifice of the individual for the community, a mystical culmination of love in violence. These thoughts he embodied in the strangest and most haunting of all his poems, *Maud*, which was published in July 1855 to be at first lamentably misunderstood by reader and critic alike. There is no reference to the book in the Royal Archives and no other evidence that the Queen or her husband read it. If

the Queen did see it, she would, no doubt, while delighting in
the love lyrics have considered the rest 'peculiar'.

But for one cause or another Royal interest in the Laureate
was undoubtedly increasing.

An opportunity to develop this came from a spring visit to
Osborne, the holiday home at the east end of the Isle of Wight,
which had given the Queen and her family so delightful an
escape from the fuss and publicity of Palace and Castle for the
past twelve years. At the west end of the island, about 15 miles
away, was Farringford where Tennyson was now living with
Emily and his two little boys, Hallam and Lionel, aged four
and two. He had taken the place furnished in 1853, with some
trepidation, as he feared that, though the house was reasonably
small, the 20-acre park, the delightful gardens and wooded
wilderness, might prove expensive to maintain. In fact he had
been overborne by the seclusion of the place, half buried in its
sheltering copses, and by the superb view from the great
French windows of the drawing-room looking over Freshwater
Bay, along the rose-pink cliffs of Afton and Brooke, to Niton
and St Catherine's Point 15 miles away. Now the continued
sales of *In Memoriam* had encouraged him to buy the place.
In the first flush of May the wild daffodils were dancing under
the elm-trees in the park, cowslips and oxlips dotted the
meadows, and primroses and violets glowed on the banks and
under the hedgerows. Indoors redecoration was in progress and
Alfred's furniture was stacked, in process of unpacking, along
the corridors and about the floors of the unfurnished rooms.

The events of this and the days following are thus delightfully described in extracts from Emily Tennyson's diary:

13th May, 1856

In the midst of all our confusion while all imaginable things
strewed the drawing room and the bookshelves were bare and
the chairs and tables dancing Prince Albert came. He had
driven over suddenly from Osborne. The parlour-maid went to
the front door, heard the Prince's name announced and being
bewildered by the confusion in the house and not knowing
what to do with 'His Royal Highness' stood stock still, so

Colonel du Plat, we hear, took her by the shoulders and turned her round. One of the gentlemen with the Prince gathered a large bunch of cowslips which the Prince said he must take himself and give to the Queen. One dropt and I kept it for the children as a memorial. A nightingale was singing while he was here, I think. It had been singing delightfully all the morning close to the house . . . The Prince said on leaving Farringford 'It is such a pretty place that I shall certainly bring the Queen to see it'.

17th May, 1856

We have a message from Lambert telling us to expect the Queen, for orders for her reception had been given at Yarmouth and one of the carriages was to be in readiness to take H.M. to Freshwater, and the Prince had said to the Captain on leaving Farringford 'it is a pretty place, it is a pretty place. I shall certainly bring the Queen to see it.' We dressed our children in their rose-coloured dresses and all went into the Farringford garden to receive H.M. etc. not liking to go into the house though we did have rugs spread on the narrow path left between packages in the entrance hall. However the Queen *did not* come probably because of the stormy morning.

20th May, 1856

I spent my Louy's birthday [Emily's sister] partly in writing letters, partly in expecting the Queen, for orders had again been received at Yarmouth 21st, 22nd and 23rd also. Captain Crozier told us that the Prince had put the cowslips in water meaning to make cowslip tea of them for himself and the Queen.

But the Queen never came and Tennyson's personal introduction to his Sovereign was once more deferred.

Very soon after this Tennyson set off, with his family, on a tour in Wales, to gather information and atmosphere for the story of Geraint and Enid which he was preparing for inclusion in the first instalment of the *Idylls of the King*. He had made careful preparation for this tour, studying the works of the bards with the aid of a Welsh dictionary. Everywhere he went he hunted up a schoolmaster or other local scholar who could help him with the language and go with him to places of legendary interest. In almost every village there seemed to be an aged harper who would play Welsh airs for him and talk of the ancient lays and ballads.

The following lines, written during the tour, in a metre approximating to the Cywddan of the famous fourteenth-century Welsh poet David ap Gwilym, show how much the Queen was still in Tennyson's thoughts.

HARP, HARP

Harp, harp, the voice of Cymry,
 Voice, whose music yet prevails,
Honour to the Head of Britain,
 Honour to the Queen of Wales.
Speak, speak, thou land of Aedd,
 Land of stream and mountain peak,
Land of Arthur and Taliessin,
 Land of old Aneurin, speak.
Speak, speak ye mountain voices,
 Cataracts breaking down the vales,
Caer Eryri, Cader Idris,
 Honour to our Queen of Wales!
Hers, hers the men of Cymry,
 High on hill or low on plain,
Praying God to guard and guide her,
 Guide and guard her long to reign.
Red, red the blood of Cymry
 Flows thro' all her mountain-dales,
Red with life and rich in loyalty
 Runs the noble blood of Wales.

This poem was not published until it appeared in *The Poems of Tennyson* (Longmans 1969), and was not sent by Tennyson to the Queen.

In June 1857 Tennyson did send the Queen a copy of the Pre-Raphaelite illustrated edition of his poems of 1842 and received a polite acknowledgment from the Lord Chamberlain '. . . The Queen desires the Lord Chamberlain to assure Mr Tennyson of Her appreciation of this attention and of the value which Her Majesty shall attach to this Book, and the illustrations so worthy of it.'

The next Royal message was no doubt less welcome. Just

before Christmas 1857, Tennyson received from the Queen, through Sir C. B. Phipps, a request for an additional stanza to 'God Save the Queen' to be sung at the State Concert which was to be given at Buckingham Palace on the evening of the wedding-day of the Princess Royal to Crown Prince Frederick William of Prussia.

However, the request could not be refused and, with creditable promptitude, Tennyson sent two stanzas for the Queen to choose from. The following note in his handwriting, preserved at Lincoln, is probably a note or draft for the letter with which he sent the stanzas to Sir Charles Phipps.

'It appeared to me that Her Majesty would like the expression "Rose of May" none the less for its being Shakespeare's: but if it seems in any way out of place this reading might be substituted.

> *Let both the Peoples say,*
> *God be thy strength and stay!*
> *God bless thy marriage day!*
> *God bless the Queen!*

If this version be adopted, then, to avoid sameness of phrase, the second line of stanza 1st should begin "Long be" or "So be" –'

Sir C. B. Phipps replied on December 29th, transmitting the Queen's thanks and continuing, 'Her Majesty thinks that it will be better to have sung both the verses which you have sent to me – the first both as bearing upon the international view of the subject and introducing the name of the Prince – the Bridegroom, and the second as more in allusion, and complimentary to the Princess Royal.

'The Queen would be sorry to lose the classical allusion so well introduced of the "Rose of May" – and which the name attached to the portrait of the Princess seems to render very apposite.'

Both Tennyson's stanzas were sung at the concert and published in *The Times* for January 26th, 1858 (see *Memoir*, i, 423), as follows:

God bless our Prince and Bride!
God keep their lands allied,
  God save the Queen!
Clothe them with righteousness,
Crown them with happiness,
Them with all blessings bless,
  God save the Queen!

Fair fall this hallow'd hour,
Farewell our England's flower,
  God save the Queen!
Farewell, fair rose of May!
Let both the peoples say,
God bless thy marriage-day,
  God bless the Queen!

This no doubt was the kind of commission which Tennyson
dreaded, and the trouble which he took to comply with it is
significant, as is the Queen's satisfaction with the result.

Tennyson now set about the completion of the projected
first instalment of the *Idylls of the King*. There were to be four
of these (afterwards re-arranged as five – 'The Marriage of
Geraint', 'Geraint and Enid', 'Merlin and Vivien', 'Lancelot
and Elaine' and 'Guinevere'). Nine years of married life had
changed very little his shyness and sensibility. Many friends
heard him recite the poems or read them in MS., including the
Duke of Argyll who was now very closely associated with the
Court. All were enthusiastic and urged prompt publication, yet
Tennyson could assure the Duke 'I so thoroughly nauseate
publishing that I could well be content to be silent for ever';
and when the Duchess, meeting him up in London on publishing business, asked him if he would like to come to an important
literary breakfast which she was planning, his reply was
immediate and unequivocal: 'Duchess, I should hate it'. However his sensibility did not prevent him (or perhaps it was due
to Emily) from arranging a first edition of 40,000 copies.
Publication took place at the end of June 1859. Success was
instantaneous – 10,000 copies were sold during the first week
and the critics were almost universally favourable.

Among the most ardent admirers of the volume was Prince Albert.

It does not appear that the poet sent the Queen a copy of the book; at least there seems to be no such copy at Windsor today, but a few months later he was delighted to receive the following letter from the Prince Consort.

Buckingham Palace
17th May, 1860

My dear Mr Tennyson,

Will you forgive me if I intrude on your leisure with a request which I have thought some little time of making, viz. that you would be good enough to write your name in the accompanying volume of your 'Idylls of the King'? You would thus add a peculiar interest to the book, containing those beautiful songs, from the perusal of which I derived the greatest enjoyment. They quite rekindle the feeling with which the legends of King Arthur must have inspired the chivalry of old, whilst the graceful form in which they are presented blends those feelings with the softer tone of our present age.

Believe me always yours truly,

ALBERT

Tennyson of course complied, and the signed copy of the *Idylls* is still in the Royal Library at Windsor.

The Queen also read the poems and shared Albert's admiration. A few days later she wrote to the Princess Royal in Germany. 'I have just been reading Tennyson's *Idylls of the King* which I think you would delight in. They are so very peculiar, quaint and poetic. 'Enid' I think quite beautiful, and the latter part of 'Elaine' very touching, 'Guinivere' very fine – the early part quite sublime'.[1]

Next to *In Memoriam, Idylls of the King* was destined to play the chief part in bringing about that unique relation between sovereign and Laureate which was to follow the tragedy of Albert's death on December 14th, 1861.

[1] *Dearest Child,* ed. Fulford (Evans Bros, 1964).

CHAPTER FOUR

QUEEN VICTORIA

THE five years following the cessation of the Crimean War were full of political trouble for the Queen, arising first out of the Indian Mutiny of 1857 and then from the threat of European war over the struggle for Italian Unity. They also brought a full share of personal troubles and anxieties.

On April 14th, 1857, her ninth and last child, Princess Beatrice was born, and on January 25th, 1858, her eldest child, Victoria, Princess Royal, was married, while still less than eighteen years old, to Frederick William, who would one day be King of Prussia. This marriage had been arranged two years before in pursuance of Prince Albert's cherished aim of a Germany united under a constitutional Prussian Monarchy. It aroused the suspicions of the French Emperor and was not popular in England, where Prussia was regarded as an insignificant German principality. The Queen, though very fond of Prince Frederick William and fully sharing Albert's enthusiasm for the match, dismissed as absurd the demand from Berlin that the wedding should take place in that city – 'whatever may be the usual practice of German Princes, it is not every day that one marries the eldest daughter of the Queen of England.'

A fortnight before she had written to her uncle, King Leopold of Belgium, 'Tomorrow is the eighteenth anniversary of my blessed marriage, which has brought such universal blessings on this Country and Europe. For what has not my beloved and perfect Albert done? Raised monarchy to the *highest* pinnacle of *respect*, and rendered it popular beyond what it ever was in this country.'

Princess Victoria (Vicky) was very like her father in character and abilities and the parting, which the Queen also felt severely, caused him intense mental anguish.

The Queen was also much agitated at this time by the desire to find a suitable husband for Princess Alice, her third child, then nearly fifteen. The choice ultimately – and very happily – fell on Prince Louis of Hesse-Darmstadt.

But the Prince of Wales (Bertie) caused his parents more anxiety than all the rest of their children. The Queen desired desperately that he should grow up a worthy successor to her adored Albert, and of course the only way to ensure this was to make him as like Albert as possible. Tutors were carefully chosen for him and rigorously instructed. Short spells were arranged for him at Oxford ('That old monkish place which I have a horror of,' the Queen called it) and Cambridge, under conditions designed to stimulate his desire for instruction and protect him as far as possible from temptation. He was sent abroad with judiciously selected bear-leaders. In fact, as some sympathetic philistine observed, everything was arranged for the poor boy, except the opportunity to enjoy himself.

The culmination of this stage of his up-bringing was a North American tour, lasting from July 10th to November 15th, 1860, in the course of which the young Prince opened a railway bridge over the St Lawrence River, laid the foundation stone of the Federal Parliament building at Ottawa, and was lavishly entertained at Washington and other great cities of the United States.

Except for some anti-Catholic riots in Canada, for which he was in no way to blame, the tour was an immense success. All were delighted with the Prince's bubbling high spirits and inexhaustible vitality. He danced until five o'clock in the morning, was with difficulty restrained from crossing over Niagara Falls on the high wire in Blondin's wheelbarrow, and showed no sign of the blasé indifference which so distressed his father and mother, and which was no doubt chiefly due to the excessive expectations which he knew that they held in regard to him.

An important item in his parents' plans for him was an early marriage, which they hoped would help him to settle down. After much anxious thought and careful consideration of all possibly suitable candidates, the choice fell upon sixteen-year-old Princess Alexandra of Schleswig-Holstein, a young lady whose great beauty and simple charm carried the day, in spite of the strong probability that the connection would put the Queen and the British Government in a very awkward position, if the clash between Denmark and Prussia over Schleswig-Holstein became serious, as it was likely to do.

All these anxieties weighed heavily on Prince Albert, making him seem older than his years. He was still only just over forty, but hard work and anxiety were beginning to tell on him. Though the Queen still spoke of him as 'the most beautiful being on earth', he was growing fat and bald and suffered from constant rheumatism and gastric troubles. Yet he could not relax or refuse even the mass of routine and social work that was thrust upon him. In May 1860 he wrote to Vicky comparing himself to the donkey which works the tread-mill at Carisbrooke Castle. 'He, too, would rather munch thistles in the Castle moat . . . small are the thanks he gets for his labour'. On October 1st he had a carriage accident, having to jump from a runaway four-in-hand. The injuries which he sustained were not serious, but his old friend Baron Stockmar, who saw him immediately afterwards, realised that he had no longer the stamina to survive a severe illness.

Queen Victoria, with her robust nature, was less perceptive. In the following February (1861) when Albert was suffering severely from toothache, she wrote to Vicky '. . . dear Papa never allows he is any better or will try to get over it, but makes such a miserable face that people always believe he is very ill. His nervous system is easily excited and irritated and he's so completely overpowered by everything. It is quite the contrary with me always. I can do anything before others and never shew it, so people never believe I am ill or ever suffer.'

The year 1861 was a momentous one for the Western World. January 9th saw the first shot fired in the American Civil War.

On the 18th February there met at Turin the new Parliament of an Italy united except for Rome and Venetia.

For Queen Victoria the year was to be dominated by personal tragedies. On March 16th her mother, the Duchess of Kent, died at the age of seventy-five after a painful illness and a harrowing surgical operation. Victoria and Albert had been hastily summoned from Buckingham Palace to the Duchess's house at Frogmore the evening before. Next morning the Duchess died with her hand in her daughter's and Albert standing by the bed. He burst into loud sobs, picked up the Queen and carried her from the room.

The Queen's anguish is shown in the letter which she dashed off that day to her Uncle King Leopold.

My dearly Beloved Uncle,
    On this, the most dreadful day of my life, does your poor broken-hearted child write one line of love and devotion. *She* is gone! That *precious dearly beloved tender* Mother – whom I never was parted from but for a few months – without whom I can't *imagine life* – has been taken from us! It is *too* dreadful ... I held her dear, dear hand in mine to the very last, which I am truly thankful for! But the watching that precious life going out was fearful! Alas she never knew me! But she was spared the pang of parting ...
    Dearest Albert is dreadfully overcome – and well he may be for she adored him. I feel so truly *verwaist* ...'

She could not face the funeral, but stood by the wreath-covered coffin to take leave of 'those dearly loved remains – a dreadful moment'.

After the first shock of grief the past rose up to torture her. She went over and over those miserable years at Kensington, those wretched animosities of the early days at Buckingham Palace. Going through the Duchess's papers, she came across innumerable signs of affection – 'not a scrap of my writing or of my hair has been thrown away – and such touching notes in a book about my babyhood.'

How could there ever have been bitterness between herself and one who had loved her so much – one whom she had come to love so much?

She retired into seclusion at Osborne, nursing her grief. 'You are right, dear child', she wrote to Vicky on April 10th, 'I do not want to feel better', and three days later: 'Don't worry yourself about me. I love to dwell on her and to be quiet and not to be aroused out of my grief! To wish me to shake it off – and to be merry – would be to wish me no good. I could not and would not!'

Princess Alice's birthday on April 24th, which should have been so happy, for the arrangements for her marriage were almost completed, was 'the saddest I remember . . . the grief and yearning and almost despair which at times comes over me, are dreadful. I find even that gets worse than better . . . my nerves are still very bad and I suffer very much from my head, and from that dreadful sensitiveness. I think I am no better than I was three weeks ago, but I am less weak.'

At the end of the month she had to go up to London for a meeting of the Privy Council about Alice's marriage. From there she and Albert withdrew for a few days of privacy to White Lodge, Richmond, where she might have been happy 'but for the dreadful reality which constantly breaks upon my mind – and damps the possibility of any enjoyment'.

Her head was still terribly weak. 'Noise still affects it painfully and I can't occupy myself for long without getting a pain in it – and getting bewildered and confused, which is tiresome and trying . . . my poor birthday is fast approaching. How I dread it. No music (that would kill me) – No change of mourning.'

The birthday (passed at Buckingham Palace) was dreadful – 'the day of all others when one loves to have one's mother, who gave it one – with pain and suffering – near one.' But she got through it better than she expected.

Then they were back at Osborne, where poor little Prince Leopold, her delicate haemophiliac child, was lying ill with measles, until June 1st, when Albert, still harassed by innumerable obligations of which his acute conscientiousness magnified the importance, decided that they must return to London for the opening of the Horticultural Garden, 'which', wrote the Queen, 'I curse for more reasons than one'.

On June 19th, a day of sweltering heat, she got quite well through an official 'Drawing Room', her first appearance in public after her mother's death. On August 17th she and Albert visited the mausoleum at Frogmore which he had planned and designed. It was a most splendid day and 'the stillness and beauty of the whole spot – its repose and calmness were most soothing'.

Soon after this they crossed over to Ireland for a short visit. At Dublin they saw the Prince of Wales who was going through a strenuous course of military training at the Curragh.

By this time the Queen had worked herself up to an extravagant idea of the Duchess's affection – 'No one, not even dearest Papa, ever loved me as she did', she wrote to Vicky on August 25th.

Next day the party went on to Killarney and, in spite of the extreme heat and the relaxing western air, Queen Victoria responded, as always, to the marvellous beauty of the lake and mountains.

Early in September they were at beloved Balmoral. There the healing process continued. Alice and her fiancé were with them – a great joy, for Alice had by now almost taken the place of Vicky, and Louis had won the affection of Victoria and Albert as well as of their daughter. News of the Prince of Wales was reasonably good. He had gone to Berlin to visit his sister, who had arranged a very discreet 'accidental' meeting with Princess Alexandra in Speyer Cathedral. The meeting (on September 24th) seemed to have been successful, though the Queen, who had, unfortunately, thought the Prince lacking in sympathy over his grandmother's death, feared that he was too blasé and indifferent to feel a very strong liking for anybody. Princess Victoria's report was ambiguous. 'I see that Alix has made an impression on Bertie, though in his funny undemonstrative way . . . In a quarter of an hour he thought her lovely, but said her nose was too long and her forehead too low.'

However, such ambiguities could not much effect the intense pleasure which life in the Highlands always gave Queen

Victoria. The weather was good, Albert seemed well and active, twice shooting three stags in a single day, and they were able to make two of those 'Great Expeditions', which were always the climax of a holiday, walking or riding on ponies over the rough mountain-paths and being met by carriages where there was a good enough road to ensure faster progress. Only at the close of the first expedition was there an incident which brought the Queen's loss suddenly and sharply to her mind. On coming down from the mountains in the evening for the drive home, they found waiting for them the Duchess of Kent's 'sociable', a favourite carriage which she had specially bequeathed to Albert.

On October 22nd they left Balmoral for 'the dreadful return to Windsor, where everything is the same but her alone – she will be missed in a manner I dare not contemplate.'

Alas! the return heralded further disasters. Leopold had recovered from the measles, but the doctors advised a warm climate for convalescence. On November 2nd they packed him off to the South of France in the charge of seventy-year-old Sir Edward Bowater. Hardly had they arrived when Sir Edward fell ill and died and a hurried search was needed to find a successor.

On November 6th came news that Ferdinand, younger brother of Don Pedro, King of Portugal, a much loved cousin of Prince Albert's, had died of typhoid. Five days later Don Pedro was dead from the same disease. The Queen who had seen in the newspaper that the King had an attack of fever, had dismissed this as 'nothing but one of those frequent little feverish attacks that foreigners so frequently have from not attending to their stomach and bowels'. She and Albert were shattered and bewildered by the suddenness of the double blow.

On November 12th, three days after the Prince of Wales's twentieth birthday, came a letter from Stockmar telling the Queen of a rumour which was circulating on the continent of a liaison which the Prince had formed with a Dublin actress while in camp at the Curragh.

The Queen remembered the profligacy of her uncles which had so much discredited the courts of George IV and William IV. Albert had been the child of a profligate father and a broken home, while his brother, the reigning Grand Duke of Saxe-Coburg-Gotha, was described, at the time of his accession, by Henry Ponsonby, afterwards Queen Victoria's sprightly Private Secretary, as 'the father, nay the grandfather now of many of his subjects'. There was also just at this moment a fear that any scandal about Bertie might wreck the plan for the Prince's marriage to Princess Alexandra. There was even fear that the liaison might be a serious one and the real reason for his apparent reluctance to marry.

Albert waited for a few days to confirm the rumour, which unfortunately he was able to do. On November 16th he wrote his son 'a long reproachful yet forgiving letter' saying that he was too broken-hearted to see him yet, and urging him to tell the whole story, 'even the most trifling circumstances' to his 'Governor' General Bruce, who was to act as the channel of communication for the time being. The young Prince's explanations to General Bruce were candid and reassuring, his contrition evidently sincere, and he pleased his father by refusing to name the friends who had led him into the escapade. Prince Albert now wished to see Bertie at Cambridge immediately, but his engagements made this impossible. On Friday November 22nd he had to inspect the new Staff College at Sandhurst. Unfortunately it was a day of heavy rain and he came back soaked to the skin and feeling very ill. There was a crowd of week-end guests at Windsor, but on Monday the 25th he travelled by special train to Cambridge, spent the night with his son, and travelled back to Windsor next day, much relieved, but unfortunately much exhausted, owing apparently to Bertie having lost the way while they were out walking together. The Queen wrote to Vicky the day after his return that she had never seen him so low, that he had a cold and neuralgia and could not sleep and was suffering from a great depression which had increased during the last three days.

On November 29th the Prince wrote to Vicky, 'Much worry

and great sorrow have robbed me of sleep for the past fortnight. In this shattered state I had a very heavy catarrh and for the past four days am suffering from headache and pains in my limbs which may develop into rheumatism.'

These were undoubtedly, though this was not realised, the first symptoms of typhoid fever. Nevertheless he went out that day to inspect the Eton College Volunteers.

On November 30th he was suddenly called upon to deal with a serious international crisis. The American Civil War was now in full spate. Britain had taken a strictly neutral position, when suddenly a federal warship intercepted the British steamer *Trent* on the High Seas and removed from her Messrs Mason and Slidell, who were on their way as special envoys from the Confederate States to the Court of St James. On the evening of November 30th the Queen received from Lord John (now Earl) Russell a draft despatch to America, which amounted to the presentation of an ultimatum to the Federal Government. The Prince got up next morning (Sunday) at seven, and, though he could hardly hold the pen, modified the draft so as to give the Federal Government an honourable way out of their dilemma, thus probably averting what might have been a war of far reaching consequence.

This was the last time that the Prince went to his desk to work. Afterwards he sat at table through a large luncheon party, but ate nothing. Another sleepless night followed. Next morning the Queen sent for William Jenner, the famous pathologist, who had recently distinguished for the first time the germs of typhus and typhoid and had been one of the Royal physicians since early in the year.

There followed twelve days of tragic anxiety. Though one need not accept Lord Clarendon's gibe that the Royal physicians were not fit 'to attend a sick cat', one must remember that medical care and medical knowledge were very different a hundred years ago from what they are today. Sickness was cared for in the home and without trained nurses, doctors had not the professional or social status they enjoy today, and the Prince's doctors were in an exceptionally difficult position.

Only a few days before the Prince had admitted to the Queen that he did not cling to life. He was happy in his life, but if he was attacked by a serious illness he would succumb without a struggle. In addition he was worn out by hard work and by anxiety about the Prince of Wales and Prince Leopold. For days he had hardly been able to face opening his letters for fear of bad news about the boy. On the top of this the deaths from typhoid of Pedro and Ferdinand had given him a shocked horror of the disease. Though Prince Albert's doctors soon diagnosed typhoid, they dared not mention this to him or to the Queen, for fear that by word or look she might betray the fact to him. Indeed they kept encouraging her by vaguely hopeful statements.

In consequence the Queen, always determined and courageous in times of crisis, preserved her optimism almost to the last. As late as November 30th she had written of an intended move to Osborne on December 13th from 'this most tiresome – and this year to me – most distasteful place.' On December 11th she wrote to Vicky, 'The Doctors are satisfied; he holds his ground', and next day she told King Leopold that the doctors expected an improvement after the end of the third week (reckoning from November 22nd) and would not be disappointed if it did not take place until after the fourth week.

Even as late as 6 a.m. on December 13th one of the doctors came to the Queen saying there was ground for hope that the crisis was over.

One result of this was that the Queen would not summon the Prince of Wales from Cambridge, fearing that after their recent trouble this might upset his father. Perhaps also she dreaded this first meeting with the poor boy after the discovery of his Curragh escapade, for she had convinced herself that this was largely responsible for Albert's collapse. Ultimately, on December 13th, Princess Alice, who had been with her mother day and night since the onset of her father's illness, summoned the Prince on her own responsibility. Even then her message was so carefully worded that Bertie carried out a dinner engagement and arrived, full of cheerful conversation, at three o'clock in the morning of the 14th.

Nevertheless the Queen had terrible moments of doubt and depression all through these painful days. Albert was restless and the doctors allowed him to wander from room to room, she following him. By day he refused to go to bed. At night he could not sleep without ether drops. He would stare at her, strange and unsmiling, hardly seeming to know who she was. There were dreadful bouts of delirium. On December 9th the Prime Minister insisted on a specialist being brought in. The Queen reluctantly agreed, her reluctance being due partly to fear of upsetting the regular doctors, partly perhaps to fear of an unfavourable opinion. When bulletins were issued for the first time on Wednesday December 11th, she felt this as an omen of doom, and on December 13th gave up keeping her diary, which she did not resume until January 1st, 1862.

It was not until after luncheon on the 14th that Victoria truly realised the situation. Jenner then warned her that congestion of the lungs had set in, though he did not tell her that he had given up hope.

The afternoon was agonising. Albert's mind wandered and he had bouts of unconsciousness. The Queen, after much hesitation, asked him if he would see the Prince of Wales. He said he would. His children came and kissed his hand but he did not seem to know it. Afterwards he revived and asked for his Private Secretary, Sir Charles Phipps. Some of his household officers came to take their leave of him. The Queen and Princess Alice sat by the bedside with heroic self control. Once the Queen could bear it no more – she rushed out into an adjoining room and threw herself to the ground in anguish. Alice called her back. 'Oh! this is death,' cried the Queen, taking Albert's left hand. It was already cold.

At a quarter to eleven in the evening of December 14th Albert died, with the Queen holding his left hand, Princess Alice on the other side of the bed, the Prince of Wales and Princess Helena at its foot. Members of the household stood about the room against the walls; others crowded the corridors.

The sick man drew two or three long but perfectly gentle breaths and all was over. The Queen stood up, kissed him on the forehead, called out in a bitter agonising cry, 'Oh! my dear Darling', and then dropped on her knees in mute, distracted despair, unable to utter a word or shed a tear.

Sir Charles Phipps and Ernest Leiningen, son of her half brother Charles, picked her up gently and carried her out of the room.

Today, more than a hundred years after the event and in a world so fundamentally changed, one cannot hope fully to realise the effect on Queen Victoria of the Prince's death. She was a woman of violent emotions, which, even when Albert was there to help her, she often found it impossible to control. As considerably more than the merely titular head of the greatest Empire the world had ever known, she faced immense responsibilities, which she no doubt believed to be even greater than they in fact were. Her large and growing family, with every member of which she was passionately involved, presented many pressing problems, both personal and political.

For more than twenty years, the responsibilities, which in her heart she feared and shrank from, had been mainly carried for her by one in whose tireless devotion and high intelligence she had absolute trust and whom she loved with absolute abandon.

Until almost the last hour she had refused to face the possibility of his death, and, now, suddenly, he was gone, and she had to face the threat of her enormous world, unaided, in the glare 'of that fierce light which beats upon a throne'.

For two days she managed to preserve an equilibrium which astonished her household and family and was only relieved by sudden bursts of convulsive weeping. On the Monday evening she began, but did not finish a letter to Vicky.

> My darling angel's child – our First-born
> God's will be done ...

Four days later she wrote to her Uncle King Leopold from Osborne, where she had gone the day before on his suggestion.

My *own* Dearest, kindest, *Father,*

For as such I have *ever* loved you! The poor fatherless baby
of eight months is now the utterly broken and crushed widow
of forty-two! My *life* as a *happy* one is *ended*! The world is gone
for *me*! If I *must live* on (and I will do nothing to make me
worse than I am), it is henceforth for my poor fatherless
children – for my unhappy Country, which has lost *all* in losing
him – and in *only* doing what I know and *feel* he would wish,
for he *is* near me – his spirit will guide and inspire me! But oh!
to be cut off in the prime of life – to see our pure, happy, quiet,
domestic life, which *alone* enabled me to bear my *much* disliked
position, CUT OFF at forty-two – when I *had* hoped with such
instinctive certainty that God never *would* part us, and would
let us grow old together (though he always talked of the
shortness of life) is *too awful,* too cruel! and yet it must be for
his good, his happiness! His purity was too great, his aspirations *too high* for this poor *miserable* world! His great soul is
now only enjoying *that* for which it *was* worthy! And I will *not*
envy him, only pray that *mine* may be perfected by it and fit to
be with him eternally, for which blessed moment I earnestly
long . . .

Only against this background can one hope to understand
what came afterwards – the long years of seclusion, the extravagant gestures of mourning, the eccentricities of affection, and –
most important for our purpose – the friendship with Alfred
Tennyson, poet of love and loss and of

'*The faith which comes of self-control*'.[1]

[1] *In Memoriam*, cxxxi.

CHAPTER FIVE

FIRST MEETING

THE news of Prince Albert's death reached Farringford on December 15th, and it is evident from the consternation which it caused that, although they had never had speech with the Queen and only the single meeting with the Prince, Alfred and Emily Tennyson already felt a close personal involvement with the Royal couple. 'A terrible blow,' writes Emily in her diary. 'One fears for the Queen, for the nation the loss is unspeakable.' On the 16th Emily sent a messenger three miles to Yarmouth, in search of news. On the 17th she records, 'A grand and touching account of the Queen.' On the 20th news comes that the Queen has arrived at Osborne. 'Not one even of her servants on the platform, only her children and Lord Alfred Paget.'

It seems that about this time Tennyson received through Sir C. B. Phipps a message transmitting from Princess Alice, the Queen's second daughter, who had been with the Queen at the Prince's death-bed, the hope that he would be able to write something about her father.

This suggestion seriously disturbed him. His strong feeling for the Prince and his romantic devotion to the Queen and her family made him ardently desire to comply with the Princess's request. But he was not at all well at the time and his dislike of writing on a set subject made him apprehensive of failure where failure would be most distressing to him. The hastily written and heavily corrected draft of a reply in his hand, now at Lincoln, shows his perturbation. The draft, with its alternative endings, is, as nearly as it can be deciphered, as follows:

Hearing of your Royal Highness's strong desire that I should write something on the memory of the Prince Consort, I answer that at present I am unwell & the subject wh I have tried is too exciting to me, but that in my own way & at my own time I trust I may be enabled to do honour to the memory of as gracious, noble & gentle a being as God has sent among us to be a messenger of good to his fellow-creatures. We all honour him – We all love him – more and more since we lost him: there is scarce an instance in History of a person so pure & blameless – is not that some comfort to Her Majesty & Her Children, some little comfort in the midst of so great a sorrow? But I wished to say to your R. H. that when I was some three or four years older than yourself I suffered what seemed to me to shatter all my life so that I desired to die rather than to live. And the record of my grief I put into a book; & (of this book) I continually receive letters from those who suffer, telling me how great a solace this book has been to them. Possibly if by & by Your R. H. would (look into this book) consider this record it might give you some comfort. I do not know. I only know that I write in pure sympathy with your affliction & that of your R. mother –
1) & if I sin against precedent in so doing
2) & if I have seemed in any way to have violated the sanctity of your sorrow
3) & if I trouble you (have troubled you) in vain forgive as your Father wd have forgiven me.

A. TENNYSON

This letter does not appear ever to have been sent, but Tennyson seems to have got into communication with Sir Charles Phipps and discussed with him possible methods of complying with the Princess's wishes.

On December 24th, 1861, he wrote Sir Charles a letter which suggests that he had by this time determined on the form of commemoration ultimately adopted – a dedication to the Prince's memory of a new edition of the *Idylls of the King* of 1859, which was already with the printers.

Farringford
December 24th, 1861

My dear Sir,
    The Queen has my full devotion, the Princess Alice my entire

sympathy and with all sincerity I mourn their unspeakable loss.

From your own kind words – if indeed I understand them rightly – I conclude that the thing which I had intended before they reached me – will happily be that most pleasing to Her Majesty and the Princess. I had thought of consecrating an Idyll to the memory of him whom we have lost. I have tried the subject more than once, but I find it too exciting for me to accomplish anything worth preserving at present, for I have been for months unwell and under medical care, and to say the truth poetry is as inexorable as death itself.

At any rate I do trust that somehow at some time I may be enabled to speak of Him as He Himself would have wished to be spoken of – surely as gracious, noble, and gentle a being as God ever sent among us to be a messenger of good to his creatures.

I am
Yours very truly,
A. TENNYSON
(Royal Archives, Windsor R.2/6)

On the same day Alfred, Emily and their two boys, Hallam, aged nine, and Lionel two years younger, travelled the fifteen miles by road to Osborne – there was no railway at that time – presumably to record their sympathy by signing their names in the visitors' book.

Alfred immediately set about his 'Dedication'. He was determined to make it as perfect in form as he could and as perfect an expression of his sympathy with the bereaved wife. On January 7th, 1862, he was able to send the completed poem to the Duchess of Sutherland, who had been the Queen's mistress of the Robes until April 1861, and the Duchess's daughter, Elizabeth, wife of his intimate friend the Duke of Argyll, who was also closely connected with the Court. Within a week an enthusiastic letter of approval came from the Duchess of Sutherland. On receipt of this Tennyson immediately despatched the poem to Princess Alice, with the following letter.

No date

Madam,

Having heard some time ago from Sir C. B. Phipps that your Royal Highness had expressed a strong desire that I should in some way 'idealise' our lamented Prince, and being at that time very unwell, I was unwilling to attempt the subject because I feared that I might scarce be able to do it justice, nor did I well see how I should idealise a life which was in itself an ideal.

At last it seemed to me that I could do no better than dedicate to his memory a book which he himself had told me was valued by him. I am the more emboldened to send these lines to your Royal Highness, because having asked the opinion of a Lady who knew and truly loved and honoured him, she gave me to understand by her reply that they were true and worthy of him: whether they be so or not, I hardly know, but if they do not appear so to your Royal Highness, forgive me as your Father would have forgiven me.

Though these lines conclude with an address to our beloved Queen I feel that I cannot do better than leave the occasion of presenting them to the discretion of your Royal Highness.

Believe me, as altogether sympathising with your sorrow,
> Your Royal Highness's faithful
> and obedient servant
> A. TENNYSON
> (Lincoln E.T.)

The poem was, of course, the well known 'Dedication' which has ever since been printed at the beginning of *Idylls of the King*. For it, since he wished to express, with due dignity and restraint, his personal sympathy directly to a suffering woman, he chose the simplest, and perhaps (for a short poem) the most difficult form – blank verse. This was in marked contrast to the symphonic elaboration of the Wellington Ode, in which he had been voicing a national grief to a nationwide audience, on the occasion of a great public ceremonial, but the result was equally impressive.

> *These to His Memory – Since he held them dear,*
> *Perchance as finding there unconsciously*
> *Some image of himself – I dedicate,*
> *I dedicate, I consecrate with tears –*
> *These Idylls.*
> > *And indeed he seems to me*
> *Scarce other than my own ideal knight,*
> *'Who reverenced his conscience as his King;*

Whose glory was redressing human wrong;
Who spake no slander, no, nor listen'd to it;
Who loved one only and who clave to her —'
Her — over all whose realms to their last isle,
Commingled with the gloom of imminent war,
The shadow of his loss drew like eclipse
Darkening the world. We have lost him; he is gone;
We know him now; all narrow jealousies
Are silent; and we see him as he moved,
How modest, kindly, all-accomplished, wise,
With what sublime repression of himself,
And in what limits, and how tenderly;
Not swaying to this faction or to that;
Not making his high place the lawless perch
Of wing'd ambitions, nor a vantage-ground
For pleasure; but thro' all this tract of years
Wearing the white flower of a blameless life,
Before a thousand peering littlenesses,
In that fierce light which beats upon a throne,
And blackens every blot; for where is he,
Who dares foreshadow for an only son
A lovelier life a more unstain'd that his!
Or how should England dreaming of his sons
Hope more for these than some inheritance
Of such a life, a heart, a mind as thine,
Thou noble Father of her Kings to be,
Laborious for her people and her poor —
Voice in the rich dawn of an ampler day —
Far-sighted summoner of War and Waste
To fruitful strifes and rivalries of peace —
Sweet nature gilded by the gracious gleam
Of letters, dear to Science, dear to Art,
Dear to thy land and ours, a Prince indeed,
Beyond all titles, and a household name,
Hereafter, thro' all times, Albert the Good.

Break not, O woman's-heart, but still endure;
Break not, for thou art Royal, but endure;
Remembering all the beauty of that star
Which shone so close beside Thee that ye made
One light together, but has past and leaves
The Crown a lonely splendour.
                            May all love

The Queen with the Prince of Wales, the Princess Royal, Crown Princess of Prussia (standing) and Princess Alice. A photograph taken at Windsor in March 1862 by W. Bambridge.

The Prince Consort in 1856. An engraving by W. Holl after a photograph by Mayall.

His love, unseen but felt, o'ershadow Thee,
The love of all Thy sons encompass Thee,
The love of all Thy daughters cherish Thee,
The love of all Thy people comfort Thee,
Till God's love set Thee at his side again!

In these lines Tennyson by his reference to 'the gloom of imminent war', recalled the dying Prince's already described intervention in the 'Trent Case', which had probably prevented war between Britain and Federalist North America. The 'fruitful strifes and rivalries of peace' recalled the Prince's creative interest in the Great Exhibition of 1851 and the forthcoming International Exhibition for which the poet had almost completed the opening ode.

Later he altered the words 'my own ideal knight' in the sixth line to 'my King's ideal knight' because people said that King Arthur was a portrait of the Prince.

On January 16th Emily Tennyson records in her diary 'a day to be remembered by us – a letter of thanks to A from Princess Alice telling us that his lines have soothed our Queen, thank God!'

The Princess's letter had been as follows.

January 15th, 1862

If words could express thanks and real appreciation of lines so beautiful, so truly worthy of the great pure spirit which inspired the Author, Princess Alice would attempt to do it; – but these failing, she begs Mr Alfred Tennyson to believe how much she admires them, and that this just tribute to the memory of her beloved Father touched her deeply. Mr Alfred Tennyson could not have chosen a more beautiful or true testimonial to the memory of him who was so really good and *noble*, than the 'Idylls of the King' which he so valued and admired. Princess Alice has transmitted the lines to the Queen, who desired her to tell Mr Tennyson, with her warmest thanks, how much moved she was in reading them, and that they had soothed her aching, bleeding heart. She knows also how *He* would have admired them.

It is worth noticing that as late as February 11th, 1862, Tennyson did not feel sufficient confidence to send directly to

the Queen a copy of the new edition of the *Idylls* which included
the Dedication, but sent it with a very diffident letter to Sir
Charles Phipps, asking him to, present it to Her Majesty,
'with every expression of my loyal devotion' if he thought that
'a copy might perhaps not be unacceptable to Her'. A week
later Sir Charles wrote transmitting the Queen's best thanks
and asking for 'several copies of the dedication printed
separately.' One of the resulting copies was no doubt sent by
the Queen to the Princess Royal in Germany, for on February
23rd the Duke of Argyll sent Tennyson the following letter in
the Princess's handwriting and at her request.

To all who possess a quick and deep appreciation of the
beautiful, it is a pleasure too great almost to be described to
read words expressing thoughts good, true and beautiful,
which one may have thought, a hundred times, and which
one has longed to hear put into words which seem worthy of
them.

Such has always been my feeling in reading Tennyson's
Poetry! By turns I have felt pleasure, admiration and awe!
Particularly I think in the 'Idylls of the King'.

The first time I ever heard them was last year, when I found
both the Queen and Prince quite in raptures about them. The
first bit I ever heard was the end of 'Guinevere', the last two
pages, the Prince read them to me, and I shall never forget the
impression it made upon me hearing those grand and simple
words in his voice! He did so admire them, and I cannot separ-
ate the idea of King Arthur from the image of him whom I most
revered on Earth!

I almost know the 'Idylls of the King' by heart now, they
really are sublime! The subject is one which creates a peculiar
interest: and the characters so perfect, so grand; the spirit of
manliness, purity and real piety which inspires the whole,
filling me with respect and awe.

As for the dedication to the Prince, I cannot say what I feel.
Never has anything been said of that great and glorious being
more true and more beautiful, this we have all felt! Surely it
must give the author satisfaction to think that his words have
been drops of balm on the broken and loving hearts of the
widowed Queen and her orphan children.

The Duke added that the Princess had expressed the wish

to have something in the poet's handwriting – perhaps the dedication, he suggested.

Tennyson had an almost pathological dislike of copying out his poems for admirers, but with many groans he copied and sent her 'a morsel of "Guinevere" '.

Meanwhile the Queen, no doubt remembering the Prince's love of *In Memoriam*, had turned to that poem for consolation. 'Much soothed and pleased with Tennyson's "In Memoriam",' she records in her diary on January 5th. 'Only those who have suffered as I do, can understand these beautiful poems.'

On February 22nd the Duke of Argyll came to Osborne for a weekend – the Queen spoke to him a great deal 'about Tennyson and his *In Memoriam*' and asked him to tell the poet how much she loved to dwell on the poem, giving him her copy to show 'how well it was read' and how many passages she had marked – 'It will touch you, I think,' wrote the Duke to Tennyson 'that she had substituted "widow" for "widower" and "her" for "his" in the lines "Tears of a Widower" (section XIII)

> *Tears of the widower, where he sees*
> *A late-lost form that sleep reveals,*
> *And moves his doubtful arms, and feels*
> *Her place is empty, fall like these.'*

A few days later he wrote again,

'Till I see you I can't tell you all about the Queen's marking in "In Memoriam". Indeed some of them seemed so sacred that except to you I should never speak of them. Perhaps no one with less wonderful truthfulness and simplicity of character would have allowed them to pass out of her own hands, but I must now mention one which touched me very much. It was in Number XXV ("I know that this was Life") – she had written
  "So it was for 22 years"
On XXIX last line of first verse ("How dare we keep our Christmas-eve") she had written
  "We did not keep it in 1861"
I need not say that I wish to tell these things to you and Mrs Tennyson *only*, she wished me to see them that I might tell you and you alone. The second verse of LXIV "Has made me kindly

with my kind" marked by the Queen seems to express Her tenderness for others – under Her own sorrow.'

On March 25th came a letter from the Duke conveying the Queen's command to visit her at Osborne. 'In these interviews,' he wrote 'one sees Her in Her own room without any form or ceremony (unless standing can be said to be so) and what She likes is to be able to speak Her sorrow and Her love to those of whom She thinks that they can feel for or with Her.'

The Command rather alarmed Tennyson and he replied briefly but urgently.

'I am a shy beast and like to keep in my burrow – two questions – what sort of salutation to make on entering Her private room? and whether to retreat backward? or sidle out as I may.'

The Duke replied, by return and at length, as follows.

Private   *London*
March 27th, 62

My dear Tennyson,

There is no other salutation expected than a respectful bow. You will probably be shown into the *Prince's* private room (dressing-room in fact) and the Queen will enter afterwards, by another door – and if you stand near the table in the middle of the room (which is small) she will be close to you almost before you see Her. I assume that you are to see Her as I saw Her, and where I saw Her. But in any case as you have already been 'presented' at Court, no other Salutation is expected than a low bow. She retires to Her own room – when she wishes to close the interview and you have therefore no bother about *your* mode of retiring.

I must tell you, however, that if you feel a mere *bow* to be stiff and unnatural, either on first seeing Her, or on Her leaving you, you need not be afraid of kneeling down and kissing Her hand – which after all is the ordinary mode of first Presentation for everyone; and is surely more natural, expressive of reverent affection, now when She is in sorrow. She does not *expect it*, and if, from accidental position, or otherwise, you don't feel it to be easy or natural, I would not do it – But if you do feel it natural, don't be afraid of doing it – I think She likes all natural signs of devotion and sympathy. In this be guided entirely by your own feelings – All formality and mere ceremony breaks down in the presence of real sorrow, and what is *natural* is right – with Her. Don't let yourself be a 'shy beast' – and 'Come out of your burrow' – Talk to Her as you would to a poor Woman in affliction – that is what she likes best.

She dislikes very much the word 'late' applied to the Prince. But as this is a phrase which does not naturally come in in speaking I only mention it in connection with the strong reality of Her belief in the *Life presence* of the Dead. There are some bits of 'In Memoriam' which are specially soothing to Her in this matter: and if she speaks on this subject (as She is almost sure to do, directly or indirectly) your feeling in regard to it would be grateful to Her.

Do you recollect saying to me the other day in your Den/ Burrow 'Oh – *they* don't sleep' – I thought at the time how pleased the Queen would be with that exclamation –

Any more? Write to me if [you] have anything more to ask.

Ever yours

ARGYLL

(PS. in another hand, presumably that of the Duchess of Argyll)

I am very glad you are to see Her – my dear Mr Tennyson.

The visit took place on April 14th. It was Tennyson's first personal introduction to the Queen and is briefly recorded in her diary, as follows:

April 14th, 1862

I went down to see Tennyson who is very peculiar looking, tall, dark, with a fine head, long black flowing hair and a beard – oddly dressed, but there is no affectation about him. I told him how much I admired his glorious lines to my precious Albert and how much comfort I found in his 'In Memoriam.' He was full of unbounded appreciation of beloved Albert. When he spoke of my own loss, of that to the Nation, his eyes quite filled with tears.

Tennyson was so moved by the interview that he could not give a very connected account of it afterwards. From what he reported to Emily, it seems that he was standing with his back to the fire when the Queen entered and that she came and stood about five paces from him with her arms crossed, very pale and like a little statue in her self-possession. She spoke in a quiet, sweet, sad voice and looked very pretty, with a stately innocence about her, different from other women. She said, 'I am like your Mariana now,' and spoke most kindly about his work and his sympathy for her, and he remembered thanking her and saying that it made him very happy, but he could not remember afterwards what she had said. She talked of the Prince, and of Henry Hallam, Macaulay, and Goethe and Schiller in connection with him, and said that the Prince was so like the picture of Arthur Hallam in *In Memoriam*, even to his blue eyes. And when Alfred said, 'He would have made a great King,' she replied, 'He always said it did not signify whether he did the right thing or did not, so long as the right thing was done.' She spoke of *In Memoriam*, quoting the last stanza of section LI as one which had been of great comfort to her:

> *Be near us when we climb or fall;*
> *Ye watch, like God, the rolling hours*
> *With larger other eyes than ours,*
> *To make allowance for us all.*

The interview closed with Alfred saying, 'We are all grieved for Your Majesty,' and the Queen replying, 'The country has been kind to me and I am thankful.' At parting she asked him whether there was anything that she could do for him, to which he answered: 'Nothing, Madam, but shake my two boys by the hand. It may keep them loyal in the troublous times to come.'

Shortly after this visit, appeared (April 24th, 1862) Tennyson's 'Ode Sung at the Opening of the International Exhibition.' In this he had, with the express approval of the Queen, included three lines of reference to the Prince, as author of the 'world-compelling plan' –

> *O silent father of our Kings to be*
> *Mourn'd in this golden hour of jubilee,*
> *For this, for all, we weep our thanks to thee!*

At the end of May the Queen sent, through Lady Augusta Bruce, who had become one of her Ladies-in-Waiting after the death of the Duchess of Kent, some volumes of German poetry, including two by Zeller, of which she had spoken to him during the interview as having been a comfort to her, though he seems to have forgotten the fact. The books not being available in England, she had sent to Germany for them and had them specially bound. In her letter, Lady Augusta wrote: 'I am again to add that *In Memoriam* is still the only book, besides religious books, to which Her Majesty turns for comfort. Some of the earlier poems, the sadder ones especially, which the Queen knew less, Her Majesty has found solace in reading.' She had also been moved by the lines 'In the valley of Cauteretz' (written in 1861 but not published until 1864), which the Duke of Argyll had recited to her, and in which Tennyson recalled his expedition through the Pyrenees with Arthur Hallam to help the Spanish revolutionaries in 1830.

Tennyson's reactions to the letter confirm Emily's feeling that he had been so moved by the interview with the Queen that he left her with a very hazy idea of what had passed.

Farringford
June 3rd, 1862

Dear Lady Augusta,

You will think me crazy. I wrote in such haste yesterday not to lose the post that I quite forgot the main purpose of my letter – at least as far as I recollect. I fear that tho' my thanks to the Queen were of course implied in what I wrote I did not request you to present them to Her Majesty.

Will you have the kindness to do so – i.e. most dutiful and heartfelt thanks either for the loan or the gift of the books, for on recurring to your letter, I read that the Queen had commanded you to send the books that I might read them and admire what she had read and admired – now if they be only lent me I am quite horror-stricken at having assumed that they were given me – yet, I think they were given.

Will you send me a single line to let me know how this is and forgive me for troubling you.

Yours very truly,
A. TENNYSON

That the Queen had been no less moved by the meeting than

the poet himself is shown by a letter, which Lady Augusta wrote immediately after Tennyson had left the Queen's presence.

Osborne
April 14*th*, 62

Dear Mr Tennyson,

I have seen the Queen since you left and hasten to relieve your mind by assuring you that your visit to this house of mourning far from paining or agitating its sorrowing inmates, has soothed and interested them. This the Queen emphatically expressed and H.M. added that it would be Her wish that this one interview should be the prelude to others, less trying than the first –. Deprived as the Queen is by the overwhelming blow that has fallen on Her, of the society and companionship of one of the most powerful, gifted, accomplished and *communicative* of minds – H.M. feels it a true solace to be brought in contact with those in whose views and aspirations the beloved Prince sympathised, whose talents and genius He appreciated and by whom He was understood and valued – Not that the latter is a consolation the Queen has far to seek (and this recalls to me some of the words I heard H.M. address to you today but did not remind you of) for deeply the Queen feels how truly your beautiful words have found an echo in the hearts of Her people and have been the expression of the universal sentiment. It is this appreciation of Him she mourns that makes the sympathy manifested so unutterably precious and gives such depth and tenderness to the exclamation you heard, 'the country has been kind to me' . . .

Lady Augusta's impression was confirmed by a letter which Tennyson received a few days later from the Duchess of Sutherland.

While at Paris I heard from the Queen after she had seen you and she felt what seemed to her the warmth and tenderness of your heart and the greatness of your mind. Could these words be said to one who agreed more earnestly? The Queen also said she would have liked to have said and asked more.

Confirmation came from the Queen herself when on January 14th, 1863, Lady Augusta Bruce brought to Farringford, 'What is to us', wrote Emily, 'beyond price. *The Prince Consort*, a gift from the Queen with kind words written by H.M.'s own hand, also a beautiful photograph of herself and three of her children with A's lines under it "May all love &c . . ." also the prayers used at the anniversary and the Sermon preached –'

The book was a specially bound volume of *The Principal Speeches and Addresses of His Royal Highness the Prince Consort with an introduction giving some outlines of His Character.*[1] The inscription read as follows:

> To Alfred Tennyson Esquire
> who so truly appreciated
> This greatest purest and best of men
> from
> the beloved Prince's
> broken-hearted widow
> Victoria
> Osborne Dec. 9, 1862.

It was probably at this meeting that Lady Augusta indicated to Tennyson that the Queen would like him to compose some lines in honour of Princess Alexandra of Denmark, who was coming to England to marry the Prince of Wales (the marriage took place on March 5th, 1863). The Queen had become devoted to the Danish Princess. She had suffered much from what she considered the Prince's instability, which she felt had contributed to Prince Albert's collapse, and she had real hopes that Princess Alexandra's beauty, charm and common sense would help her eldest son to settle down and accept his responsibilities. Tennyson shared this hopefulness of the Queen and the Nation, and gave brilliant expression to the general feeling in the well-known 'Welcome to Alexandra' – a 'little lyrical flash, an impromptu', he called it, in a letter to the Duchess of Argyll – which was sent to the Queen on March 6th and published in *The Times* for March 10th, 1863.

> *Sea-kings' daughter from over the sea, Alexandra!*
> *Saxon and Norman and Dane are we,*
> *But all of us Danes in our welcome of thee, Alexandra!*
> *Welcome her, thunders of fort and of fleet!*
> *Welcome her, thundering cheer of the street!*

[1] John Murray, 1862.

Welcome her, all things youthful and sweet,
Scatter the blossom under her feet!
Break, happy land, into earlier flowers!
Make music, O bird, in the new-budded bowers!
Blazon your mottoes of blessing and prayer!
Welcome her, welcome her, all that is ours!
Warble, O bugle, and trumpet, blare!
Flags, flutter out upon turrets and towers!
Flames, on the windy headland flare!
Utter your jubilee, steeple and spire!
Clash, ye bells, in the merry March air!
Flash, ye cities, in rivers of fire!
Rush to the roof, sudden rocket, and higher
Melt into stars for the land's desire!
Roll and rejoice, jubilant voice,
Roll as a ground-swell dash'd on the strand,
Roar as the sea when he welcomes the land,
And welcome her, welcome the land's desire,
The sea-kings' daughter as happy as fair,
Blissful bride of a blissful heir,
Bride of the heir of the kings of the sea –
O joy to the people and joy to the throne,
Come to us, love us and make us your own:
For Saxon or Dane or Norman we,
Teuton or Celt, or whatever we be,
We are each all Dane in our welcome of thee,
*   Alexandra!*

On March 8th the Queen sent a message of thanks through Lady Augusta, who wrote:

'Her Majesty desires me to thank you very warmly and to tell you with how much pleasure she had read the lines and how much she rejoices that the sweet and charming Princess should be thus greeted.'

The day of the wedding was celebrated at Farringford by a bonfire on the down – very grand, 'with great green flames darting out along the ground, curling and licking' – the description recorded in Emily's diary must be Alfred's – and a fine torch-light procession. Hallam and Lionel stayed up to wait on the guests at supper and drink the health of the Queen and the happy couple. 'Alfred', writes Emily, 'says the simple words "The Queen and God bless her" very grandly and very impressively.'

On March 16th Alfred and Emily drove to Osborne to write their names. On returning they were much amused to find that a large number of carriages had been drawn up at Farringford gate waiting for a rumoured visit of the Prince and Princess of Wales, and had only dispersed with reluctance when assured by the household that no such visit was in contemplation.

On May 9th the whole family visited Osborne in order that the children, Hallam and Lionel now aged respectively ten and nine, might be presented to the Queen in accordance with her promise of the year before. The invitation came in response to a gift of snowdrops gathered by Hallam and sent by him to Lady Augusta for the Queen, who kept them on her dressing-table for a week and sent a message of thanks to him, saying that she was very glad that he had that name and that he had such good and great godfathers as F. D. Maurice and Henry Hallam.

Emily's diary for May 9th records the visit to Osborne in detail.

A., the boys and myself to Osborne. We lunch with Lady Augusta Bruce and afterwards drive with her in the grounds. We see the dairy. Very pretty it is, lined with white Dutch tiles with a wreath of convolvulus round and a fountain in the middle; then the kitchen where the Princesses amuse themselves with cooking, also lined with white tiles. The little garden, the fort where Prince Arthur had made [*sic*] the pet donkey that draws the gun carriage, the Swiss Cottage where they have their Museum and another where they come to tea.

Soon after we return Lady Augusta is sent for and she comes to fetch us to the Queen. We wait in the Drawing-room and after a very little time we heard a quiet shy opening of the door and the Queen came in and I kissed her hand.

She shook hands with the boys and made a very low reverence to A. All the Princesses came in by turns, Prince Leopold also.

All shook hands very kindly with us all. We had met Prince Alfred before in one of the corridors with Prince Louis of

Hesse[1] and he had shaken hands with A. and talked to him.

The Queen's face is beautiful. Not the least like her portraits but small and childlike, full of intelligence and ineffably sweet and of a sad sympathy.

A. was delighted with the breadth and freedom and penetration of her mind. One felt that no false thing could stand before her. We talked of all things in heaven and earth it seemed to me. I never met a Lady with whom I could talk so easily and never felt so little shy with any stranger after the first few minutes.

She laughed heartily at many things that were said but shades of pain and sadness passed over a face that seemed sometimes all one smile. Princess Alice joined pleasantly in the conversation and Prince Leopold and Lady Augusta talked with the boys.

One feels that the Queen is a woman to live and die for.

I am sorry that A. might not have a warm shake of the hand such as the boys and myself had when the Queen retired.

I gave Princess Beatrice A's poems because she had said to Lady Augusta that she wished A. would write her some 'poetries' that she might learn when she was a big girl. A. wrote his name in the book and the Princess's. He and the boys had some tea and Lady Augusta went off with the Queen and Princess Alice to Newport. We saw them from a balcony when they drove away. A footman came to take us on the terrace. As A. said, the grounds looked sad, the hands that had laid them out being gone.

In a letter (Lincoln) to her sister Anne Weld, written three days after the visit, Emily – while admitting that when the Queen entered the room she found herself on her knee kissing the hand that was given her, but not knowing how she got there – gave an ecstatic description of the Queen's face and expression. 'Her face is really beautiful now in its childlike simplicity . . . quite a small face, beaming all over.'

Ten-year-old Hallam described the day from a different angle.

Osborne, 9th May, 1863

We all went to Osborne on 9th May 1863. We had our dinner there with Lady Augusta Bruce and then went out driving in

---

[1] Husband of Princess Alice since July 1st, 1862.

one of the Queen's carriages. We saw a beautiful Pinus Insignis that the Prince Consort had planted in 1847 and there was a beautiful puzzle monkey at the Queen's dairy, once called and was the old Abbey of Barton. We saw the Queen's dairy. We had pretty glimpses of the sea now and then. We saw the young Princes' and Princess's gardens. There were potatoes and artichokes. There were a great many mares tail about Osborne, asparagus and radishes. We went into a Swiss cottage that the Queen had given to them as a Christmas present.

We saw fossils and birds stuffed and a wolf, very big, and a gentleman brought a fish home and a naughty little puppy tore it to pieces. We saw another Swiss cottage with an old dame of 81 in it. There the Princesses cook and all was beautifully arranged. There was another little room and in there a little shop belonging to the Princess Beatrice about a foot square and at the top [of the shop] was put Grocer Spratt to Her Majesty and Princess. Princess Royal was very fond of cooking biscuits.

Beatrice assured Lady Augusta that she served a large quantity of tea out to Her Majesty and there were really little tea caddies and tea and sugar and all sorts of good things. There was a little fort that Prince Arthur made all by himself with a very little help. It was called Victoria fort and Albert Barracks: there was a little drawbridge. There was the British flag floating gently at the top of a little flag staff and a powder recess and four or five little canons: there was a moat round the fort. Prince Arthur is destained for an engineer. We saw the pet donkey which used to draw the gun carriage. We drove back to Osborne. We went into one of the drawing-rooms. The Queen came and made a very low bow. Her Majesty shook hands with Mamma and Mamma very courteously went down on one knee and kissed the Queen's hand and the Queen shook hands with Lionel and myself and we shook hands with all the Princes and Princesses except Princess Louise: she only shook hands with Mamma. I had a chat with Prince Leopold about the South of France and Paris, he said he did not like Boulogne. The Princess Louisa asked me whether I could draw, I told her I could not. She can draw beautifully and Prince Leopold can a little: he talked about his fine ships, how he made them as follows (he makes them with paper, he put a match into one of them and it burnt beautifully, it was very windy that day: he put a match into another and it would not burn so he tied two together and they burnt beautifully. There is a little bit of the sea where it is quiet and *that* is where he sails his boats: he talks about building castles in this quiet part of the sea where he sails his boats).

The Queen wears a locket round her neck with thin black velvet. The Queen is not stout. Her Majesty has a large mind and a small body to contain it therein. We went into Lady Augusta's room and had tea. We saw Sir Charles Phipps the Secretary of the Queen, he was a very nice gentleman. (I forgot that after we came from driving we saw Prince Alfred, he looked just like a Norwegian. He shook hands with Papa and was very reverential to him and called him Sir. We saw Prince Louis of Hesse).

There was a big balustrade outside. We saw the Queen out driving. Her Majesty bowed as she passed by us on the balustrade. Her Majesty drove out with Prince Leopold, Princess Alice, Louis of Hesse and Lady Augusta Bruce. We go home and the porter at the gate smiled when we said how beautiful the Queen was. Her Majesty has a beautiful little nose and soft blue eyes. The Princesses wore dresses, light blue with black spots except Princess Beatrice who was dressed in a sort of checked light blue with a piece of black velvet to tie up her long golden hair. Papa and I saw (as we thought) Princess Beatrice's shetland pony. Princess Beatrice's cat died at seven o'clock that night.

List of Princes and Princesses whom we saw at Osborne exactly in the order we saw them –

Prince Alfred	Princess Helena
Prince Louis of Hesse	Princess Beatrice
Princess Alice	Princess Louisa
	Prince Leopold

Princess Beatrice said to Lady Augusta Bruce (not in our presence) (Guste short for Augusta) Guste why do you always call Ma 'Mam'?

Observations:–You must always say 'Mam' when in her Majesty's presence. You must stand until the Queen asks you to sit down. Her Majesty does not *often* tell you to sit down.

Finis

The Queen's diary chronicles the visit briefly but impressively.

9th May, 1863

Walking with Alice and then driving 4 little ponies. Ernest
and Marie came to luncheon.

Afterwards saw Mr and Mrs Tennyson and their 2 sons.
Had some interesting conversation with him and was struck
with the greatness and largeness of his mind, under a certainly
rough exterior.

Speaking of the immortality of the soul and of all the
scientific discoveries in no way interfering with that, he said,
'If there is no immortality of the soul, one does not see why
there should be any God,' and that 'You cannot love a Father
who strangled you', etc.

Emily's letter to her sister records that two days after this
visit a Queen's messenger came to Farringford 'with books for
Ally, "The Meditations" and Guizot's "Prince Albert", and
an Album in which Ally was asked to write a poem' – 'Ally'
tactfully chose 'In the Valley of Cauteretz' which the Queen
had praised to the Duke of Argyll and which was conveniently
short.

1864 was marked by a difficult commission, which caused
Tennyson some trouble. On January 3rd he received a letter
from the Dean of Windsor saying that the Queen would be
much pleased if he would write four lines to be put on the
statue of the Duchess of Kent, her mother, in the Frogmore
Mausoleum.

Tennyson complied with four lines beginning 'O blessing of
thy child as she was thine'. These, however, proved unacceptable and in the following letter from one of the Queen's ladies
he was very respectfully asked to try again.

Jan. 21st, 1864

Dear Sir,

The Queen desires me to return from Her hearty thanks for
the beautiful lines you have so promptly sent Her. Beautiful
as they are, your tried kindness induces the Queen to let you
know honestly that they do not quite express Her idea.

The Dean may not have explained that the Mausoleum is
divided into two parts – a lower chamber where the sarco-
phagus is placed – and a totally distinct upper chamber which

is approached by a different path and encircled by a terrace where seats are placed and flowers grow in ornamental vases and where if the Duchess had lived it was her intention often to take tea, etc. In the centre of this Gallery the statue will be placed under a cupola – the statue represents the Duchess standing in full evening costume and the Queen wishes to remember Her mother as she was in Life.

Your lines H.M. thinks would be most appropriate on the tomb itself. If you would write another verse taking for your motto 'Her children arise and call her blessed' which is more the sentiment the Queen wishes to express, Her Majesty would be extremely obliged to you – She desires me to apologise for again troubling you and

> Believe me
> yours truly
> KATHERINE M. BRUCE

Tennyson now sent the four lines which were afterwards printed by Hallam Tennyson in his *Memoir* (vol. ii, 17).

> *Long as the heart beats life within her breast,*
> *Thy child will bless thee, guardian-mother mild,*
> *And far away thy memory will be bless'd*
> *By children of the children of thy child.*

Warm approval of these lines was communicated in a further letter on Jan. 27th.

The Queen desires me to return you Her very sincere thanks for the beautiful lines you have sent Her – and for all the trouble you have taken to meet Her wishes.

I have by Her Majesty's command already sent to the Sculptor a copy of the lines beginning 'Long as the heart beats life, etc.' to be engraved on the pedestal of the statue. Her Majesty preferred this verse both from the expression 'Guardian-Mother mild' which she particularly admired, as so descriptive of the Duchess, and also because the Queen did not quite like Herself putting 'O blessing of thy Child *as she was thine*' under the image of her Mother. H.M. thought it too presuming.

Again thanking you in Her Majesty's name.

> Believe me
> Yours truly,
> KATHERINE M. BRUCE

On the statue the lines appear under an epigraph from the Book of Proverbs:

'Thy children shall rise up and call thee blessed'.

It was no doubt a sign of the Queen's increasing interest in Tennyson that he was, at the beginning of 1865, sounded through his friend Frederick Locker, Lady Augusta's brother-in-law, on the possibility of a baronetcy being conferred on him. After some hesitation, owing to his fear that his refusal might be misunderstood by the Queen, he indicated that he would not feel able to accept, and the matter was dropped.

Tennyson now regularly sent copies of his new publications to the Queen, and her diary records readings by Princess Alice and the Prince of Wales from *Enoch Arden* ('a most beautiful new poem') and by Lady Augusta of 'The Holy Grail' and 'The Golden Supper' ('very beautiful, but peculiar').

Early in 1865 Tennyson, encouraged by the great popularity of his *Enoch Arden* volume of the previous year, had a selection of his poems published serially in threepenny numbers. He sent copies to the Queen, who returned a message through one of her ladies expressing 'her cordial satisfaction on hearing that this admirable selection from your poems will thus be brought within the reach of the poorest among the subjects of Her Majesty.'

Later she records having read to herself all the four *Idylls* in the 'Holy Grail' volume (1870). 'Pelleas and Ettare' she finds 'very fine but not a very pleasing subject' and 'The Passing of Arthur' 'most moving and written long ago with the addition of a short introduction'.

The four years following the Tennyson family's visit to Osborne were very busy years for Queen Victoria, politically as well as domestically. She still maintained her determination to avoid all purely social and ceremonial activities, almost the only function of this kind which she was willing to undertake being the unveiling of statues of Prince Albert, which, as Mr Gladstone remarked, 'soon covered the land'. But she devoted herself unsparingly to what she considered her political duties as sovereign. Though she could not be, like Prince Albert, an informal member of all governments, she felt it her duty to keep herself fully informed on all political questions of importance, and to communicate her views emphatically and clearly to her Ministers. She recognised that the final decision must be left to them, but she also felt it her duty to make it quite clear to them when she felt their decisions to be wrong.

As Albert had done, she took particular interest in Foreign Affairs, making it her principal aim to follow up what she knew to have been his policies – particularly his desire to see Germany united under the leadership of a progressive Prussia. The application with which she mastered complex questions and the clarity of her conclusions show that her willingness to leave political questions to Albert had not been due to lack of capacity.

The problems which most troubled Europe during the years 1863–7 arose out of the struggle between Prussia and Austria for the control of the German States, and the struggle between the German States and Denmark for the control of the Duchies of Schleswig-Holstein. The Schleswig-Holstein question was of incredible complexity, fully justifying Lord Palmerston's gibe that there had only been three people who had really understood it: the Prince Consort, and he was dead; a German Professor, and he had gone mad; and himself, and he had forgotten all about it. The Queen applied herself with such determination to this singularly arid problem that her understanding of it often staggered those who ventured to discuss it with her. Her position in regard to it was complicated by the marriage of the Prince of Wales to Princess Alexandra, daughter of the King of Denmark, one of the claimants. The Princess was very popular in Britain and both the Liberal Government, then in power, and popular opinion strongly favoured Denmark as a small nation fighting against heavy odds. The Queen, however, was strongly influenced by her German connections and by Prince Albert's idea of a united Germany under Prussian leadership. She took refuge from her dilemma in a policy of strict neutrality. In August 1863 she visited Germany, partly to see once more the scenes of Prince Albert's boyhood, partly to discuss European problems with the King of Prussia, Vicky's father-in-law, and the Emperor of Austria, Franz Josef.

On February 1st, 1864, the Prussian and Austrian army crossed the river Eider, prepared to drive the Danes out of the contested Duchies. Three days later the Queen insisted on the modification of the speech from the Throne prepared for her by the Prime Minister, because she considered it too bellicose in tone. The Danes were soon defeated, and the British Government, with her approval, arranged for a conference to be held in London on April 20th to discuss the situation. The Queen herself saw many of the delegates personally, urging mutual concessions and speaking to all with great freedom. When the conference proved abortive, she continued her pressure for strict neutrality, often going well beyond what would now be considered proper for a constitutional sovereign.

In spite of all her efforts Austria and Prussia resumed hostilities and soon occupied the whole of the Duchies. But the division of the spoils brought the conquerors into conflict with one another. War broke out between them, and, as a result of the Prussian Victory at Sadowa on July 3rd, 1866, Austria was driven out of the German Confederation and Prince Albert's ideal of a Germany united under Prussian Leadership brought nearer to realisation, though not by methods which he would have approved, for Prussia's success involved the annexation of the ancient kingdom of Hanover, which had given Britain its Royal family. Queen Victoria saw with regret the retirement to Paris of her first cousin, the blind King George, son of the Duke of Cumberland, with his daughter Princess Frederika, and the loss of much territory by her son-in-law the Grand-Duke of Hesse-Darmstadt, husband of Princess Alice.

Her distress was increased by the death at the end of 1865 of her Uncle, King Leopold of Belgium, to whose sagacity and experience she had so often been indebted since and even before her accession.

The resumption of the correspondence with Tennyson after all these distractions was due to his initiative.

On January 28th, 1867, he sent Sir Thomas Biddulph, who had succeeded Sir Charles Phipps as one of the Keepers of the Privy Purse, a copy of his 'Elaine' with illustrations by Gustave Doré, which Messrs Alexander Strahan had recently published. In asking Sir Thomas to present it to the Queen, Tennyson made it clear that he did not much like the volume, finding the illustrations not very true to the text, and the form of the book to represent the taste of the publisher rather than his own. However 'Elaine', a masterpiece of Victorian sentiment about the lily maid of Astolat's death for love of Sir Lancelot, was a favourite of the Queen's, and almost by return came a 'command' to Alfred and Emily for a visit to Osborne, with a choice of dates between February 7th and February 20th. Emily, who was just recovering from illness and had not yet been out, did not feel well enough to go, so the poet set off with Benjamin Jowett, who was staying at Farringford and offered to go with him – though not of course into the Royal presence.

Emily afterwards described the interview in a letter to her father and her sister, Anne Weld.

My dearest Daddy and Nanny,
    I hope that the interview went off well though the conversation was not so interesting apparently as in the others he has had, but it did not flag.
    Mrs Gordon was there, Caroline Herschel who was, and Ally was glad to see her again. She is coming here, she said.
    Ally made the Queen laugh when speaking of the Cockneys and our farmhouse rooms. She said that we are not much troubled here and Ally said, 'Perhaps I should not be either if I could stick a sentry at my gates.'
    She enquired as to what was doing in poetry. Ally told her of Browning and of Swinburne and added 'but verse writing is the common accomplishment in the world now, every one can write verses. I dare say Y.M. can.' Upon which the Queen said 'No – that I cannot. I never could make two lines meet in my life.'

They talked about hexameters, Herschel's translation of the Iliad naturally introducing them, about Doré, the French, Ally's book, which she thought so handsome that apparently her object in sending for him was to thank him for it.

She said that she liked Queen Emma[1] very much and remarked how Lady-like she is.

Ally burst forth into indignation at the rich British people who could do no more for her than 4000 instead of the 40,000 she wants. (I hope this may do her some good.)

The Queen asked Ally why he did not do some great work. He said that it was such an age and they talked about the age. Ally said he feared Universal Suffrage and vote by ballot would be the ruin of us.

She asked about the boys, said that she had heard Marlborough was the best school. She bid Ally to express Her regret that I could not come.

I hope I have not tired you, but I thought that you would like to have some little idea of the visit. Ally did not see any of the Princes or Princesses, only Sir Thomas Biddulph who received him at the door and Capt. de Roos and a silent maid of Honour whom he did not know who stood by during the interview. I know you will not mention what I have said. Things get so repeated.

Eleven months later the Queen brought out her first publication *Leaves from the Journal of our Life in the Highlands.* Emily's Journal for January 20th, 1868, records: 'The Queen's book on the Highlands comes with a kind inscription to A. He reads some of it to us. Touching records of a happy simple life.' This copy is at Lincoln. It is inscribed:

> Alfred Tennyson Esquire,
> Trusting he will
> not criticise too severely
> from
> Victoria R. Osborne, January 18, 1868

Lincoln also has a copy inscribed by the Queen:

[1] Queen Emma of the Sandwich Islands, who had come to England to raise money for the building of a cathedral in her country and had visited Tennyson at Farringford in the autumn of 1865.

To her Poet Laureate
Alfred Tennyson
from Victoria R. I.
Feb. 1877.

The next few years saw the longest interruption of the
Queen's contact with her Poet Laureate. For her these were
years of much distraction.

1868 was the first year of Gladstone's first Premiership,
which caused her many misgivings, though relations between
the two were still relatively peaceful. In this and the succeeding
year she was much occupied in mediating between the Government and the opposition on the passage of two Bills, with
which she herself was not particularly sympathetic but which
seemed likely to provoke dangerous conflicts between the
Commons and the Lords, the Reform Bill (which became law
in 1868) and the Bill for the disestablishment of the Irish
Church. Then in 1870 came the Franco-Prussian war, which
broke out just after the Mordaunt divorce case in which the
Prince of Wales had been involved as a witness. During the
summer and autumn of 1871 the Queen had a bad illness in the
course of which she lost two stone in weight. On November
21st, while she was still convalescent, the Prince of Wales was
stricken with an attack of typhoid, which nearly proved fatal.
It was not until February 27th, 1872, that she was able to
attend a service of thanksgiving for his recovery, in St Paul's
Cathedral. The next day a sixth attempt was made on her life
by a weak-minded youth called Arthur O'Connor.

And this was not all. The years 1867–83 were years of great
political activity but they were also the years of John Brown.

Brown had been Queen Victoria's personal ghillie and groom
at Balmoral from about 1858, when he was twenty-four years
old, but his name does not become prominent in her diary until
the autumn of 1863. In October 1864 it was decided to bring
him down to Osborne for the winter to encourage the Queen in
her riding, which she was inclined to let drop. In the following
February she decided that he should continue permanently as
her personal attendant, making himself useful in other ways

besides leading her pony. From this time the Queen's dependence on John Brown increased from year to year, until, as she said to the Minister at Crathie near Balmoral after his death, 'He became my best and truest friend as I was his.'

As the years passed this friendship became the subject of much gossip, ribaldry and misunderstanding. In 1866–7 there were world-wide rumours that the Queen was Brown's mistress or that they were secretly married. These rumours died down in time, but misunderstandings and jealousies continued, leading to much trouble in the Royal household. The Queen, however, held on her way, and in the end Brown's position was accepted both at home and even on her visits abroad.

No doubt it was difficult for her contemporaries to understand the Queen's position – probably she did not understand it very clearly herself. John Brown gave her, what it must always be difficult for a reigning sovereign to enjoy, a direct human relationship on a different level from that on which she met her Ministers and courtiers – different even from that on which she met her own family. As Sir Henry Ponsonby, her very human and percipient Private Secretary, observed, she found in Brown something that medieval monarchs found in their Court jesters. He treated her as a woman – indeed some times, to the dismay of her courtiers, he addressed her as 'wumman'. He understood her weaknesses and didn't pretend not to see them. He understood her need for affection and support, and in his rough and genuine way gave her both. Moreover, as Strachey acutely observed, 'The power of a dependant still remains, by a psychological sleight of hand, one's own power, even when it is exercised over oneself. When Victoria meekly obeyed the abrupt commands of her henchman to get off her pony or put off her shawl, was she not displaying, and in the highest degree, the force of her volition? This was the way in which it pleased her to act and there was an end of it.'

It is surely significant that the last and much the most intimate phase of Tennyson's friendship with the Queen began with the letter of sympathy which he wrote to her in 1883 on Brown's death.

In a sense and in part, Tennyson, during this last phase, filled Brown's place. He too met her on a different level from Court and family, though not on the John Brown level. He could never have called her 'wumman', but he instinctively understood her spiritual needs and spoke directly to them with sympathy, and with that extraordinary simplicity and earnestness, which sophisticated people were apt to find embarrassing.

Henry Irving once said that Tennyson was the most 'natural' person he had ever known 'as natural as a great Newfoundland dog,' and Henry James, meeting him for the first time in 1877, was struck by his swarthiness and scragginess and the simplicity and rusticity of his speech and manner, 'like a creature of some primordial British stock'. Queen Victoria too was a 'natural'. When the two met one deep called to another.

The renewal of correspondence after the meeting of 1867 was again due to Tennyson's initiative. He had been deeply moved by the Prince of Wales's serious illness in 1871, following so quickly on the Queen's long indisposition. He was also much incensed by the development of the little England movement which had recently found expression in an article in one of the leading newspapers, urging that Canada should sever her connection with the Mother Country as being 'too costly' for British resources.

The preparation of the first Collected Edition of *Idylls of the King* seemed to provide an admirable opportunity for a public expression of personal sympathy with the Queen and of political principles which he knew she would approve. The *Idylls* had, ever since Prince Albert's letter of May 17th, 1860, been a strong link between Tennyson and the Royal family. His dedication of 1862 had been the first step in the development of the sympathetic and intimate relationship which had grown up between the Queen and himself. Messages from the Queen and the Princess Royal had in 1868 spurred him on to tackle (successfully) the subject of the Holy Grail, his difficulties over which had been the main cause of the ten-year interval between the publication of the first and second instalments of the series. Now, with the publication of the second instalment in 1869–70 and the addition of 'Gareth and Lynette' and 'The Last Tournament' in 1872, the work seemed to have reached what might be its final form, and Tennyson was just printing the collected *Idylls of the King* in Strahan's 'Library' Edition of his Works. He now decided to add to the volume a dedicatory Epilogue 'To the Queen'. He sent her a copy of this in advance and received a very cordial message of thanks through Lady Augusta[1] – now the wife of A. P. Stanley, the distinquished Dean of Westminster. Tho' the Epilogue is, of course, well known it will be convenient to reprint it here.

TO THE QUEEN

O loyal to the royal in thyself,
And loyal to thy land, as this to thee –
Bear witness, that rememberable day,
When, pale as yet, and fever-worn, the Prince
Who scarce had pluck'd his flickering life again
From halfway down the shadow of the grave,
Past with thee thro' thy people and their love,
And London roll'd one tide of joy thro' all
Her trebled millions, and loud leagues of man
And welcome! witness, too, the silent cry,
The prayer of many a race and creed, and clime –
Thunderless lightnings striking under sea
From sunset and sunrise of all thy realm,
And that true North, whereof we lately heard
A strain to shame us 'keep you to yourselves;
So loyal is too costly! friends – your love
Is but a burthen: loose the bond, and go.'
Is this the tone of empire? here the faith
That made us rulers? this, indeed, her voice
And meaning, whom the roar of Hougoumont
Left mightiest of all peoples under heaven?
What shock has fool'd her since, that she should speak
So feebly? wealthier – wealthier – hour by hour!
The voice of Britain, or a sinking land,
Some third-rate isle half-lost among her seas?

[1] Lady Augusta, though no longer a member of the Queen's household, remained her friend and confidante.

There *rang her voice, when the full city peal'd*
Thee and thy Prince! The loyal to their crown
Are loyal to their own far sons, who love
Our ocean-empire with her boundless homes
For ever-broadening England, and her throne
In our vast Orient, and one isle, one isle,
That knows not her own greatness; if she knows
And dreads it we are fall'n. − But thou, my Queen,
Not for itself, but thro' thy living love
For one to whom I made it o'er his grave
Sacred, accept this old imperfect tale,
New-old, and shadowing Sense at war with Soul,
Ideal manhood closed in real man,
Rather than that gray king, whose name, a ghost,
Streams like a cloud, man-shaped, from mountain peak,
And cleaves to cairn and cromlech still; or him
Of Geoffrey's book, or him of Malleor's, one
Touch'd by the adulterous finger of a time
That hover'd between war and wantonness,
And crownings and dethronements: take withal
Thy poet's blessing, and his trust that Heaven
Will blow the tempest in the distance back
From thine and ours: for some are scared, who mark,
Or wisely or unwisely, signs of storm,
Waverings of every vane with every wind,
And wordy trucklings to the transient hour,
And fierce or careless looseners of the faith,
And Softness breeding scorn of simple life,
Or Cowardice, the child of lust for gold,
Or Labour, with a groan and not a voice,
Or Art with poisonous honey stol'n from France,
And that which knows not, ruling that which knows
To its own harm: the goal of this great world
Lies beyond sight: yet − if our slowly-grown
And crown'd Republic's crowning common-sense,
That saved her many times, not fail − their fears
Are morning shadows huger than the shapes
That cast them, not those gloomier which forego
The darkness of that battle in the West,
Where all of high and holy dies away.

As soon as the printed volume was available Tennyson sent a

copy to the Queen, who on February 26th replied in her own hand, though still writing in the third person.

Though Lady Augusta Stanley has already conveyed the expression of the Queen's warmest thanks for and high admiration of the beautiful epilogue he has so kindly inscribed to herself she wishes to repeat again herself to Mr Tennyson these feelings on the occasion of the arrival of the copy of the very fine new edition of the 'Idylls of the King'.

Pray accept the renewed thanks of the Queen for the noble heart-stirring words addressed to her, and which were a complete surprise. It would give the Queen much pleasure could she, some day, when he is within reach of Windsor, show him the Mausoleum She has raised over the earthly remains of her dear Husband whom he knew how to appreciate, and so beautifully described, as she feels sure he would admire it and think it worthy of Him who wore

The 'White flower of a blameless life'.

She also hopes that Mr Tennyson will not find Osborne too far a drive from Freshwater.

This letter (the first written to him in the Queen's own hand) reached Tennyson when he was in London on business. Two days later Lady Augusta wrote asking whether he could come to Windsor the following week to visit the Mausoleum. The invitation was most unwelcome, for he was longing to get home and had just refused an invitation to visit the Rothschilds at Tring to meet the historian Motley. He wrote, with unusual irreverence, to Emily. 'How I wanted to shirk it, so I said deuce take all Kings and Empresses and deuce take the Bruce, but I suppose I shall have to go and stop here till I go.'

The visit took place on March 6th, 1873, and, as usual when he was with the Queen, there was a complete absence of awkwardness and constraint and a completely satisfying communion of personalities. The Queen's diary records the meeting as follows.

March 6, 1873

. . . Drove down to the Mausoleum with Beatrice and the Dss. of Roxburghe, & met the Dean, Augusta S. & Tennyson. He got up on the steps to look at the dear beautiful statue.

When I showed him some of the details of the decorations in the building he said the whole effect was very beautiful & worthy of what it was intended for. I observed that it was light and bright, which he thought a great point & went on to say that he wished funerals could be in white! Why should death, which was already so dreadful in itself, be clothed with every-thing to make it worse, as if it were the end of all things ? . . .

One result of this very successful meeting was that Tennyson was again sounded (through Lady Augusta) as to whether he would accept a baronetcy. This suggestion, after an unsuccess-ful effort to get the honour conferred on his eldest son, Hallam, instead of on himself, he ultimately declined.

Before the end of the year Tennyson was approached again with a request which at first he found far from congenial.

Prince Alfred Duke of Edinburgh had for some time been wanting to marry the Grand Duchess Marie, grand-daughter of Czar Nicholas I of Russia, against whom we had fought the Crimean War. His mother did not at all welcome this match. She disliked and distrusted the Romanovs, saw no political advantage in the marriage and doubted whether the Duke would make a good husband. The engagement, which was announced in July 1873, was the prelude to much diplomatic and domestic irritation and it was not until late in the year that the Queen became reconciled to it by the warmth and spontan-eity of the young Grand Duchess. The wedding was to be in St Petersburg in January 1874, and before the end of the year she asked Lady Augusta to find out whether Tennyson would be willing to compose an ode for the occasion. Lady Augusta's letter to the Queen of March 4th, 1874, shows the course of the negotiations.

I have the inexpressible pleasure and honour of forwarding to your Majesty Lines which will I am sure give Your Majesty pleasure and call for Your Majesty's admiration – Tennyson did not feel, when we saw him before Xmas, that he could put his thoughts into a harmonious shape – and Your Majesty knows how impatient of all considerations but the breathing of the Gods his muse is, at least how very little at his own com-mand or under his own control.

Our surprise and delight were equal when we heard three days ago that he had felt able to write and we have been waiting impatiently for the arrival of the M.S. which, as it turns out, had been addressed to me and mislaid for two days owing to my being out of the way. I have kept a copy. Will Your Majesty sanction my sending it to the Empress. I think it could not but please her? – I daresay Your Majesty will allow Mr Tennyson to hear, if, as I feel sure, Your Majesty approves and is pleased to accept the Poem.

(Royal Archives, Windsor, S.29/15)

*'A Welcome to Her Royal Highness
Marie Alexandrovna, Duchess of Edinburgh'*

I

*The Son of him with whom we strove for Power –
Whose will is lord thro' all his world-domain –
Who made the Serf a man and burst his chain –
Has given our Prince his own imperial flower*
Alexandrovna.

*And welcome Russian flower a people's pride
To Britain, when her flowers begin to blow!
From love to love from home to home you go
From mother unto mother, stately bride,*
Marie Alexandrovna!

II

*The golden news along the Steppes is blown,
And at thy name the Tartar tents are stirr'd;
Elburz and all the Caucasus have heard:
And all the sultry palms of India known*
Alexandrovna.

*The voices of our universal sea
On Capes of Afric as on cliffs of Kent,
The Maories, and that Isle of continent
And loyal pines of Canada, murmur thee,*
Marie Alexandrovna.

III

*Fair empires branching both in lusty life! –
Yet Harold's England fell to Norman swords;
Yet thine own land has bow'd to Tartar hordes
Since English Harold gave its throne a wife*
Alexandrovna.

For thrones and peoples are as waifs that swing,
And float or fall, in endless ebb and flow;
But who love best have best the grace to know
That Love by right divine is deathless king,
                              Marie Alexandrovna.

IV

And Love has led thee to the stranger land
Where men are bold and strongly say their say; –
See, Empire upon Empire smiles today,
As thou with thy young lover hand in hand
                              Alexandrovna.

So now thy fuller life is in the west,
Whose hand at home was gracious to thy poor:
Thy name was blest within the narrow door;
Here also, Marie, shall thy name be blest
                              Marie Alexandrovna.

V

Shall fears and jealous hatreds flame again,
Or at thy coming, Princess, everywhere,
The blue heaven break, and some diviner air
Breathe thro' the world and change the hearts of men
                              Alexandrovna?
But hearts that change not, love that cannot cease
And peace be yours, the peace of soul in soul!
And, howsoever this wild world may roll
Between your peoples, truth and manful peace,
                              Alfred–Alexandrovna.
                    (Royal Archives, Windsor, S.29/16)

The five years that followed were a period of great emotional
conflicts for the Queen. 1874 saw Disraeli's second Premiership
followed by the rapid development of her intense personal
feeling for him and her intense antagonism to his great rival,
Gladstone. Under Disraeli's influence she began to take more
part in public life than she had done during the preceding
twelve years of her widowhood. In 1876 she was proclaimed
Empress of India. The years 1875–7 were disturbed by the
dangerous conditions in the near East, which ultimately led
to the Russian-Turkish War and the triumphant return of
Disraeli (now Lord Beaconsfield) from the Congress of Berlin.
In these events she was passionately, and indeed turbulently,

interested. Tennyson meanwhile, already sixty-five years old,
was engaged in the beginning of his ten-year struggle to
establish himself as a poetic dramatist. It is not surprising
therefore that there is once more an interruption of correspondence. Again the resumption seems to have been due to the
poet's initiative and to domestic events in the Royal family,
which powerfully moved his sympathy. On December 14th,
1878, Princess Alice died in piteous circumstances. Five years
before she had lost her little son, Prince Frederick William, as
a result of injuries which he had sustained in 1873 through a
fall from a window under his mother's agonised gaze. In
November 1878 her eldest child, Victoria, afterwards wife of
Louis of Battenberg (Marquess of Milford Haven), went down
with diphtheria. Two days later the terrible disease struck her
little Alice (who was to recover and become the wife of the
ill-fated Nicholas II of Russia) and then in quick succession
the baby (Mary Victoria), Irene, Ernest (the only son),
Elizabeth and the Grand Duke himself. On November 16th
the baby died and on the 22nd Prince Ernest was thought to
be dying. His distracted mother, seeking to comfort and
encourage him, did what she had been told most urgently to
avoid – she took him in her arms and kissed him. By the 25th
Prince Ernest was out of danger, but within a fortnight his
mother had developed the disease, and on December 14th, the
anniversary of the death of her father, at whose bedside she
had watched with her mother seventeen years before, she too
died. This terrible blow aroused Tennyson's deepest sympathy,
for the dead Princess had been closely associated with him
during those early months of his first introduction to the
Queen. The extraordinary fortitude with which the Queen
withstood the blow, added to his sympathy. She refused to
postpone the date of the Duke of Connaught's wedding, fixed
for the beginning of March 1879, and herself broke the dreadful news to those of her children who were within personal
reach. In the issue of the *Nineteenth Century* for April 1879,
Tennyson published, with his famous ballad, *The Relief of
Lucknow,* a 'Dedicatory Poem to the Princess Alice'

Dead Princess, living Power, if that, which lived
True life, live on – and if the fatal kiss,
Born of true life and love, divorce thee not
From earthly love and life – if what we call
The spirit flash not all at once from out
This shadow into Substance – then perhaps
The mellow'd murmur of the people's praise
From thine own State, and all our breadth of realm,
Where Love and Longing dress thy deeds in light,
Ascends to thee; and this March morn that sees
Thy Soldier-brother's bridal orange-bloom
Break thro' the yews and cypress of thy grave,
And thine Imperial mother smile again,
May send one ray to thee! and who can tell –
Thou – England's England-loving daughter – thou
Dying so English thou wouldst have her flag
Borne on thy coffin – where is he can swear
But that some broken gleam from our poor earth
May touch thee, while remembering thee, I lay
At thy pale feet this ballad of the deeds
Of England, and her banner in the East?

Tennyson does not seem to have approached the Queen directly before publishing this poem, but through Dean Stanley and Theodore Martin, who was in close touch with her over the Life of the Prince Consort which he was preparing, he ascertained that nothing which he proposed to say would be distressing or distasteful to her.

The Queen's views ultimately reached the poet, rather tortuously, through the following letter to Theodore Martin from one of the Ladies of the Bedchamber.

Windsor Castle
March 2nd, 1879

My dear Mr Martin,

I was obliged to ask the Queen about the Grand Duchess, for the question has been so much discussed. Her Majesty was most kind and desired me to say that they know Her Royal Highness kissed little Princess Mary after her death and Prince Ernie says, his mother kissed him repeatedly, but the Grand Duchess never told the Queen nor the Grand Duke so the Queen

Inscription in Queen Victoria's hand in The Principal Speeches and
Addresses of His Royal Highness The Prince Consort.
It reads 'To Alfred Tennyson Esq Who so truly appreciated this greatest, purest
and best of men from the beloved Prince's broken-hearted Widow Victoria Reg.
Osborne Dec: 29. 1862'.

O loyal to the royal in thyself,
And loyal to thy land, as this to thee —
Bear witness, that remembrable hour, morn
When pale from fever yet the goodly Prince.
Who scarce had pluck'd his flickering life again
From halfway down the shadow of the grave,
Past with thee Thro' thy people & their love,
And London roll'd one *tide* of joy thro' all
Her trebled millions, & loud leagues of man
And welcome: witness too, the silent cry.
The prayer of many a people, creed & clime —
Thunderless lightnings striking under sea
From sunset & sunrise of all thy realm,
And that true North, whereof we lately heard
A strain to shame us ' keep ye to yourselves,
& For here we sicken of your loyalty:
Your love is as a burthen; get you gone?'
Is this the tone of empire? *this the faith*
That *we* made us rulers? this, indeed, her voice
And meaning, whom the roar of Hougoumont
Left mightiest of all peoples in the West?
What shock has fool'd her since, that she should speak
So feebly? — wealthier - wealthier - hour by hour.
The voice of Britain, or a sinking land,
Some thirdrate isle half-lost among her seas?
There rang her voice, when the full city peal'd
Thee & thy Prince! the loyal to their crown
Are loyal to their own far sons, who love
Their ancient Ocean-empire, & her throne

A manuscript of Alfred Tennyson's epilogue to the Idylls of the King
(see page 89)

thinks it might be lightly mentioned but not touched upon. I hope you will forgive me having asked the question as it is best to know exactly what the Queen thinks and wishes.

Yours truly,

JANE ELY

The year 1879 saw Tennyson's first personal introduction to the Princess of Wales. This took place at the house of Mrs Sabine Greville, sister-in-law of Sir Dighton Probyn, Master of the Prince's Household. The Princess asked him to read aloud to her the 'Welcome to Alexandra' which he had written in her honour sixteen years before. This he did with his usual gusto. Then he dropped the book and both of them burst into uncontrollable laughter, suddenly struck with the absurdity of the situation.

There is no evidence that the Queen was in any way responsible for Tennyson's next Laureate utterance – the lines which he wrote in connection with the marriage at Windsor on April 24th, 1880, of Princess Frederika of Hanover, romantically known as 'The Lily of Hanover', to Baron von Pawel-Rammingen. The old blind ex-King had died in Paris in the middle of 1878. Frederika, whom Prince Alfred, Duke of Edinburgh, had once wanted to marry, had been the constant companion of her father until his death, and it seems probable that Tennyson got to know her after the King's death had taken place, for there are at Lincoln two letters of the year 1879 from her thanking him for presentation copies of his works, one of which mentions the pleasant day which she had spent at Aldworth – probably that autumn – and an invitation to repeat the visit.

Early in the next year, 1880, the daughter of an old and valued friend of the poet was appointed Lady in Waiting to Princess Frederika. This was Constance, fourth daughter of Sir John Joshua Guest, by his second wife, *née* Lady Charlotte Bertie, who after Sir John's death in 1852 had married Charles Schreiber, M.P. for Cheltenham and Poole. Lady Charlotte was a very remarkable woman – a fine Welsh scholar and a learned collector of British ceramics, fans and playing-cards, her important accumulations of which she ultimately presented to the nation. Tennyson had used her translation of the Welsh *Mabinogion* for his Geraint Idylls, and several of his poems had been printed at the Guests' private press at Canford Manor, Dorset.

Early in April 1880 Constance, who had married the Hon. Charles Eliot, a son of the Earl of St Germans, came with the Princess to Farringford, and it seems from her letter of April 19th to Hallam Tennyson that she then urged him to persuade his father to write some lines for the Princess's forthcoming marriage.

Albert Cottage, Osborne, Isle of Wight
April 19/80

My dear Hallam

Thank you very much for your note. The Princess enjoyed Her visit to F. v. much and was none the worse for it. We had a lovely passage back.

The only kind of thing to connect Her and Her Father was that thro' Her devotion to Him, she [*sic*] simply supplied His great want – in fact Her eyes were His and Her love for her Father, which was very great, made a beautiful medium thro' which He saw all the wonders of nature and no one was more worthy of these beauties than He was. In return He stored her mind with that knowledge of literature and music which He possessed in no small degree and so opened the eyes of Her mind that the result is visible in the large heart full of noble sympathy and unselfish kindness which is one of her particular charms. I do not think I am wrong in thinking that there cannot be anything more touching in Her life with His [*sic*] to form a subject worthy of a few lines on her marriage written by one who knows so well as your Father does how to put pathos into verse.

I hope to go to London soon, and that I shall see you.

Yours affectionately,

CONSTANCE R. ELIOT

You were forbearing with me and my 15-years-ago sentimentality on Thursday. It was rather ridiculous, I own, and yet one hated to be always cold and reserved and forgetful apparently of the joys of other days. The Princess was delighted with Her 'crockery'.

The pathos of the situation and the impulsive and romantic charm of the advocate must have had a powerful effect for the lines (afterwards published in *Ballads and Other Poems*, C. Kegan Paul & Co., 1880) arrived in time for the wedding which took place only five days after the date of Constance's letter.

'TO PRINCESS FREDERICA ON HER MARRIAGE'

O you that were eyes and light to the King till he passed away
From the darkness of life –
He saw not his daughter – he blest her:
The blind King sees you today,
He blesses the wife.

CHAPTER SIX

THE LAST PHASE

ANOTHER three years were to elapse before Tennyson's friendship with the Queen entered on its last and most intimate phase. On April 19th, 1881, to Queen Victoria's great grief, Lord Beaconsfield died, after losing a general election to Gladstone in the previous year, and she was involved during the next six years in intermittent bickering with her old antagonist – particularly over Afghanistan, Ireland, Egypt and the Sudan. Then on March 29th, 1883, ten days after she had sustained a heavy fall which brought on a succession of painful rheumatic attacks, her faithful servant John Brown, on whom she had, since the Prince Consort's death, grown to depend more than on any one else, suddenly died in the prime of life. The blow to the Queen was heavy. It seems from Victoria Baillie's letter of August 2nd, which is quoted below, that Tennyson wrote her letters of sympathy both after her accident and after John Brown's death. As a result of these she appears to have sent him a message through Sir Henry Ponsonby indicating that if he could come to Osborne she would be very glad to see him. His reply of May 6th, 1883, shows that he was not well enough to act on Sir Henry's suggestion.

Dear Sir Henry,

I thank you for your kind transmission of the Queen's words and I much regret not having been able to drive to Osborne for the probable chance you named of seeing Her Majesty, but since my return from Town I have not been well enough to undertake so long a drive against the east wind. I can only hope that the improvement in H.M.'s health has been so great as the most loyal of her people can desire.

Perhaps it may interest the Queen to see the Quatrain on Caxton's motto which I have written at the request of Archdeacon Farrar for the memorial to the old printer in St Margaret's Westminster.

Therefore I send it. Show it or not as you think best.

(Lincoln, Princess Louise)

The Caxton Epitaph (afterwards published in *Tiresias and Other Poems*, Macmillan, 1885) was based on convictions which Tennyson knew that the Queen shared with him, and no doubt he hoped that the indirect reference to these would be an unobtrusive source of consolation to her.

'EPITAPH ON CAXTON'

FIAT LUX (his motto)
Thy prayer was 'Light – more Light –
While Time shall last!'
Thou sawest a glory growing on the night,
But not the shadows which that light would cast,
Till shadows vanish in the Light of Light.

On August 2nd Victoria Baillie, a niece of Lady Augusta Stanley who was now a Lady in Waiting, wrote to Hallam Tennyson from Osborne.

Osborne
August 2nd, 1883

My dear Hallam,

The Queen has desired me to write to ask whether it would be possible for your Father to come over here from Aldworth – Of course he is not to do it if it is likely to be too much for him, but H.M. would so much like to see him if he could manage it. You would of course come with him.

The Queen was so very much pleased with the letters Mr Tennyson wrote to Her after Her accident, and the loss of Her old servant, and she has been reading *In Memoriam* again with such pleasure, which has made Her wish to see Mr Tennyson again.

Please let me hear as soon as you conveniently can, whether it would be a possible undertaking.

Her Majesty also requests me to say that if Mr Tennyson

could come, she would see him in Her own room without any form.

Please give my best love to Mr Tennyson.

Ever yours very sincerely,

VICTORIA BAILLIE

In response to this invitation Tennyson immediately travelled from Aldworth to the Isle of Wight and on August 7th saw the Queen at Osborne. No record by him of what passed at this interview has been found, but there are two versions of an account of the meeting in her *Journal*. One of these she sent to Hallam Lord Tennyson on October 19th, 1892, after his father's death (see p. 144) and one is in the not always exact copy of the diary made by Princess Beatrice when the original diary was destroyed after the Queen's death. Of the two versions the former is obviously to be preferred and it is therefore printed below with the addition of the eight words in italics, which the Queen, in transmitting the copy evidently left out as likely to give pain to the family, but which occur in Princess Beatrice's copy.

Osborne
Tuesday, Aug. 7th, 1883

After luncheon saw the great Poet *Tennyson* in dearest Albert's room for nearly an hour; – and most interesting it was. He is grown very old – his eyesight much impaired *and he is very shaky on his legs*. But he was very kind. Asked him to sit down. He talked of the many friends he had lost and what it would be if he did not feel and know that there was another World, where there would be no partings; and then he spoke with horror of the unbelievers and philosophers who would make you believe there was *no* other world, no Immortality – who tried to explain *all* away in a miserable manner. We agreed that were such a thing possible, God, who is Love, would be far more cruel than any human being. He quoted some well-known lines from Goethe whom he so much admires. Spoke of the poor Lily of Hanover so kindly – asked after my grandchildren. He spoke of Ireland with abhorrence and the wickedness in ill using poor Animals.[1] 'I am afraid I think the world

[1] Refers to the maiming and burning of cattle in the Irish agrarian troubles. Cf. 'Locksley Hall: Sixty Years After' (1886).

is darkened, I daresay it will brighten again.'

I told him what a comfort *In Memoriam* had again been to me which pleased him; but he said I could not believe the number of shameful letters of abuse he had received about it. Incredible! When I took leave of him, I thanked him for his kindness and said I needed it, for I had gone through so much – and he said you are so alone on that 'terrible height, it is Terrible. I've only a year or two to live but I'll be happy to do anything for you I can. Send for me whenever you like.' I thanked him warmly.

The correspondence which resulted from this meeting is difficult to reconstruct owing to the probable loss of one or more letters and the absence of dates on some others.

The Queen's letter of August 14th, which seems to have been the first written to him in the first person, was probably not the first of the series, as the opening paragraph suggests that she had already received a letter from Tennyson dealing with a question which cannot now be identified.

Osborne
August 14th, 1883

I have to thank you so very much for giving yourself the trouble of attending to the question which puzzled me and others very much. The 2nd suggestion was just what I wished to express.

Let me now say how much gratified and interested I was to have seen you again and to have conversed so freely with you on subjects of such importance.

I felt deeply touched by your kindness to me and your true sympathy! I *do* need it, for few have had more trials and *none* have been or still are in such an exceptionally solitary and difficult position. It has been my anxious wish to do my duty to my country, though politics never were congenial to me and while my dear Husband lived I left as much as I could to Him. Then when He was taken I had to struggle on alone. And *few know what* that struggle has been!

Friends have fallen on all sides and, one by one, I have lost those I cared for and leant on most. And now again lately, I have lost one who humble though he was – was the truest and most devoted of all! He had *no* thought but for me, my welfare, my comfort, my safety, my happiness. Courageous, unselfish, *totally* disinterested, discreet to the highest degree, speaking the truth fearlessly and telling me what he thought and considered to be 'just and right', without flattery and without saying what would [be] pleasing if he did not think it right – and *ever* at hand – he was *part* of *my life* and quite invaluable!

He has been taken and I feel again very desolate, and forlorn – for what my dear faithful Brown – for he was in my service for 34 years and for 18 never left me for a single day – did for me, no one else *can*. The comfort of my daily life is gone – the void is terrible – the loss is irreparable! The most affectionate children, no lady or gentleman can do what he did.

I have a vy [*sic*] dear devoted child who has always been a dear unselfish companion to me, but she is young and I can't darken her young life by my trials and sorrows. My other children, though all loving, have all their own interests, and homes. And a large family is a great anxiety.

God will I trust give me strength to the end when I trust to meet again those I have 'loved and lost' but only for a while.

You were so kind that I have let my pen run on and said more than I intended when I first began my letter, but I wished to let you know what I felt unable to *say* to you the other day.

I have preferred writing in the first person, as the other form is so stiff and it is difficult to express feelings in the third person.

My dear Beatrice returned well this morning to my great comfort and much regrets not having been here when you came.

Trusting to see you you again and wishing to be remembered to Mrs Tennyson

Believe me
Yours   v.r.i.

Tennyson's letter, dated August 1883, seems to be a reply to the Queen's of August 14th.

August 1883

Dear and honoured lady, My Queen,

Your Majesty's letter made me glad that even in so small a matter I may have been of some service to you. I will not say that I am 'loyal' or that your Majesty is 'gracious' for these are old hackneyed terms used or abused by every courtier, but I *will* say that during our conversation I felt the touch of that true friendship & sympathy which binds human beings together, whether they be Kings or cobblers.

Madam, when I left your presence, those lines of our Shakespeare in his *Henry Vth* came across my memory.

> *O hard condition! Twin-born with greatness . . .*
> *What infinite hearts-ease must Kings neglect*
> *Which [sic] private men enjoy!*

So it is, but I trust that in spite of the loneliness of the throne and your Majesty's many losses, and this latest of your faithful servant, the return of your beloved daughter may be of some solace to you.

I remember dear Princess Alice bringing her to me in the drawing room at Osborne – a fair-haired child whom it was a pleasure to look upon.

My wife is very grateful for your Majesty's most kind remembrances and

I am always
your affectionate servant
A. TENNYSON
(Lincoln, E.T.)

Balmoral Castle
August 28th, 1883

You have written me a very kind letter for which I am truly grateful. You say that you are glad to be of service to me. I am, therefore encouraged to ask your help again.

Years ago you wrote some beautiful lines for my beloved Mother's Statue, which are engraved on the pedestal.

Could you help me in choosing one or two lines to be put on the pedestal of the bronze statue of my faithful attendant and friend which is to be placed in the grounds here in a pretty quiet spot? as well as a small granite drinking fountain which I am placing to his memory in Frogmore Gardens near the small cottage where I used so often to sit in summer?

Perhaps you may like to know what is on the stone where what is earthly of him rests and I enclose the transcription.

The words (besides the Text) are by Robertson, taken from his Life not his Sermons. –

The characteristic to be remembered in any inscription like those I named above are: – Power, Strength, and moral as well as physical, truth, devotion, unselfishness.

My dear Child has returned strong and well from Aix-les-Bains which is a great blessing.

I so much regret you did not see my dear grand daughter – dear Alice, sweet girl.

Trusting that I am not indiscreet and do not take undue advantage of your kindness.

Believe me always
Yours truly,
V.R.I.

Enclosure

This stone is erected
In affectionate and grateful
remembrance of
The devoted & faithful Personal Attendant
And Beloved Friend of
Queen Victoria
In whose service he had been for 34 years
Born at Crathienaird 8th Dec. 1826
Died at Windsor Castle 27th March 1883.

'That friend on whose fidelity you count
That friend given you by circumstances
Over which you have no control,
was God's own gift.'

*   *   *

Well done! good and faithful servant,
thou hast been faithful over a few things,
I will make thee ruler over many things,
enter thou into the joy of thy Lord.

Tennyson replied from Aldworth in a letter of which the date does not survive, sending the Queen four alternative suggestions.

Madam,

I have in compliance with Your Majesty's wish sent all the quotations, which occurred to me, and which seem to bear upon the subject. I fear that no one of them may exactly suit, but perhaps the single line from Pope is the best for the purpose, since though it misses some of the characteristics of J.B. no record can go beyond 'the noblest work of God.'

Believe me always
Your Majesty's devoted servant,
A. TENNYSON
(Royal Archives, Windsor, Z.211/24)

The first line might be omitted.

> (O good old man! how well in thee appears)
> The constant service of that antique time [*sic*]
> When service sweat for duty not for meed!
>
> SHAKESPEARE

> Friend more than servant, loyal, truthful, brave!
> Self less than duty, even to the grave!
>
> ANON

> A truer, nobler, trustier heart
> More loving and more loyal never beat
> Within a human breast.   BYRON

> An honest man's the noblest work of God.
>
> POPE
> (Royal Archives, Windsor, Z.211/25)

The Queen replied accepting the anonymous lines which she rightly divined to be by Tennyson himself. Lady Longford (*Victoria R.I.* p. 452) describes them as 'singularly gawky'. But Tennyson evidently knew what the Queen wanted and they are at any rate entirely truthful and free from sycophancy.

> *Balmoral Castle*
> *Sept. 15th, 1883*

I have to thank you very much for your kind letter and the quotations. I have chosen the second beginning

'Friend more than Servant' which every one thought is very applicable.

Is it not perhaps by yourself? It struck me as so very fine.

Byron's is very beautiful too, and will admirably suit one of the other memorials.

The last by Pope is truly grand in its simplicity but in this case we wanted a little longer inscription.

I know not if the papers speak the truth in saying you are cruising with Mr Gladstone.

With renewed thanks,

> Ever
> Yours truly,
> V.R.I.

I send this note to Mrs Tennyson.

The reason for the Queen's postscript was that on September 8th Tennyson had left with Gladstone on a trip to Scandinavia in the 4000-ton steamer of the 'Castles' line, *Pembroke Castle*, which Sir Donald Currie had put at their disposal. In the course of this trip they visited Copenhagen, where Tennyson declined, on the plea of old age, an invitation to dine with the King and Queen of Denmark, but very much enjoyed a luncheon party on the ship at which they were guests with the Princess of Wales and the Czar and Czarina who were all staying at the Royal Palace. The Queen was much incensed with Gladstone for going, without warning her or seeking permission, to visit the Danish Court, where the Czar was staying, at a time when our relations with other European Powers, especially France, were in rather a delicate state, but she evidently did not allow this to affect her feeling for Tennyson.

Immediately on getting back to Aldworth, Tennyson wrote, on September 22nd, an acknowledgement of the Queen's letter of the 15th.

Madam,
Our cruise was so unpremeditated as to direction that my wife could not forward Your Majesty's letter to me, but could only place it in my hand just after my arrival at home yesterday evening.

I need not say that I have great pleasure in learning that the quotations suggested by me have been approved by Your Majesty and that the accompanying lines have been considered applicable. I feared that they were too elliptical.

The sight of the Princess of Wales in the midst of her own family, all of whom seem so royally simple and kindly was, I think, the pleasantest thing that occurred in our whole voyage, delightful as it was, for the longer I live the more I value kindness and simplicity among the sons and daughters of men.

Believe me, Madam,
Your Majesty's loyal and affectionate servant,
A. TENNYSON
(Lincoln, Identical copies A.T. & E.T.)

During the voyage home from Copenhagen Gladstone had

offered Tennyson a Peerage.[1] This, after considerable hesitation, he had accepted. He had an immense respect for the House of Lords, where of course the parties were much better balanced than in recent times, considering it foremost in debating power, and a stable, wise and moderating influence in a changeful democratic age. But he knew that he would never be able to take any active part in the proceedings of the House, and shrank from the introduction of a new and troublesome element into the last years of his life, accompanied, as he knew it would be, by jealous and malicious attacks of a kind which he found particularly distressing. On the other hand the idea of a hereditary honour which would enable his heirs (and particularly Hallam, who had given up all idea of an independent career to help his father) to take an active part in the government of the country appealed to him strongly. He also, of course, was anxious to fall in with the Queen's wishes. He therefore accepted Gladstone's offer and on his return wrote as follows to the Queen.

Madam,
    I have learned from Mr Gladstone Your Majesty's gracious intention toward myself, and I ask to be allowed to express to your Majesty my grateful acknowledgements.
    You, Madam, who are so full of sympathy for your subjects will, I am sure, understand me when I say that the knowledge of Your Majesty's approval of what I have been enabled to do is as far as I am myself concerned all that I desire.
    This public mark of your Majesty's esteem which recognizes in my person the power of literature in this age of the world, cannot however fail to be gratifying to my nearest and dearest.
                        I am, Madam, always your Majesty's
                             faithful subject and servant
                    (Royal Archives, Windsor, R.53/126)

To this the Queen replied in a letter to which she signed herself 'Yours Most sincerely' instead of 'Yours truly', as hitherto in her first-person letters.

---

[1] There seems to be no evidence that the Queen knew in advance of this offer though it is hard to believe that she did not. The correspondence between the Queen and Gladstone on the subject will be found in *The Queen and Mr Gladstone*, Philip Guedalla, vol. II, pp. 245–8 (Hodder & Stoughton, 1913).

Balmoral Castle
October, 2nd, 1883

Dear Mr Tennyson,

I thank you sincerely for your two last kind letters.

It affords me much pleasure to confer on my Poet Laureate, who is so universally admired and respected, a mark of my recognition of the great services he has rendered to literature which has so great an influence on the World at large.

How I wish you could suggest means of crushing those horrible publications whose object is to promulgate scandal and calumny which they invent themselves!

The anonymous lines you sent me are admired by everyone who sees them and will be engraved on the Pedestal of simple unpolished Balmoral granite on which stands the statue of the brave, kind, good, honest man whom they so truly describe.

Hoping to see you in the course of the next few months.

> believe me always,
> Yours
> Most sincerely,
> v.r.i.

On February 12th, 1884, the Queen published *More Leaves from a Journal of our Life in the Highlands* and sent a copy to her Poet Laureate with a characteristically realistic letter.

Osborne
(undated)

Though a very humble and unpretending author I send you my new book which perhaps you may like to glance at. Its only merit is its simplicity and truthfulness.

What a warm winter we have had! –

Hoping that you are well and wishing to be kindly remembered to Lady Tennyson,

> Ever
> Yours truly
> v.r.i.

This copy, inscribed by the Queen 'To her Poet Laureate Lord Tennyson from Victoria R.I.' Feb. 13, 1884 is at the Lincoln centre which also has a copy inscribed by the Queen 'To Lady Tennyson from Victoria R. I. Balmoral Nov. 2. 1894'.

Tennyson's acknowledgement was at once tactful and sincere.

Farringford

Madam,

This beautiful morning has brought me the pleasant surprise of your Majesty's most gracious letter and gift.

I need scarcely assure you, Madam, of my gratitude at receiving the Volume from Your Majesty's own hands.

If I may venture to say so, I am certain beforehand of finding the lofty and tender sentiments and the hearty enjoyment of nature expressed in pure English which cannot fail to make a book interesting apart from the special interest which must of necessity belong to this particular volume.

My wife is most grateful for Your Majesty's gracious remembrance.

Allow me, Madam, to subscribe myself

Your Majesty's
devoted and affectionate servant,
TENNYSON
(Lincoln E.T.)

On the day before the first anniversary of John Brown's death, March 28th, 1884, the Queen was shocked by a telegram announcing the death of her youngest son, Leopold Duke of Albany, in his thirty-first year, while his wife was awaiting the birth of their second child. Though restless, wilful and sometimes difficult to handle, Leopold had brains and energy, was better read than most of the family and took a great interest in politics. He had been born with haemophilia, the then mysterious bleeding disease, and his health had always been a source of great anxiety to his mother, who had rejoiced in his marriage in April 1882 and the birth of his child. 'The dearest of my dear sons', she called him in those first agonising days after his death.

Tennyson immediately (on March 29th) wrote a letter of sympathy.

Farringford

I cannot refrain from expressing the profound sympathy felt by myself and all mine with Your Majesty in this great sorrow.

Most anxiously do we look for news of your Majesty, fearing the effect of this sudden and terrible blow.

We are sure that your Majesty will for the sake of the poor

young widow, whom your own sad experience will enable you to comfort better than any other human being, fight against the prostrating influence of a mother's grief. Also your Majesty will not forget that you are now more than ever deeply rooted in the hearts of your People, who pray God to comfort you with the assurance that a life so full of promise has not been lived in vain here and is ever advancing toward higher fulfilments *there*.

Your Majesty's affect^{te}. and loyal servt.

TENNYSON

(Royal Archives, Windsor, R.12/67)

At the same time he wrote some lines which Hallam Tennyson, in the second volume of his *Memoir*, p. 437, says were sent to the Queen. There is a copy in Hallam's handwriting in the Royal Archives (RA Add. A.17/747) as follows.

> *Early-wise, and pure and true,*
> *Prince, whose father lived in you,*
> *If you could speak, would you not say:*
> *'I seem, but am not, far away;*
> *Wherefore should your eyes be dim?*
> *I am here again with Him.*
> *O Mother-Queen, and weeping Wife,*
> *The Death, for which you mourn, is Life!'*

Immediately on the receipt of Tennyson's letter the Queen wrote a touching reply, which however only reached him a fortnight later for reasons explained by Princess Louise in her letter of April 12th.

Windsor Castle
March 31st, 1884

I truly value your very kind words.

My sorrows are many and great!

Almost all I needed most to lean on – and who were helps and comforts – are taken from me! But though *all happiness* is at an end for *me* in *this* world – I am ready to fight on, praying that I may be supported in bearing my heavy cross – and in trying to be of use and help to the poor, dear young widow of my darling child, whose life which was so bright and happy for barely 2 years, has been utterly crushed! But she bears it admirably and with the most gentle patience and courageous unmurmuring resignation.

All those terrible sorrows show us however, truly and really, that this is not our abiding Home!

Still it is very hard to see such a young life, so full of Talent, so gifted, so useful, cut off so soon, and to feel that all the care and anxiety which under Providence enabled him to attain full manhood – was unavailing at last. –

I am well, and while I live will devote myself to the good of my dear Country who has on all occasions of sorrow or joy, but especially the former, shown such sympathy with me!

Ever
Yours truly,

V.R.I.

Windsor Castle
April 12th, 1884

Dear Lord Tennyson,

The Queen desires me to send you the enclosed letter, and to say that she is distressed to find that through some oversight of one of her gentlemen, owing to the great press of business the letter was misdirected and thus the delay.

The Queen was much touched by your beautiful letter to her, and had hoped you would have received her letter some days ago.

The Queen is well but the blow is a heavy one and only by degrees will she realise what she has lost in that beloved son who has been taken from her.

I do not like to tell you of my own sorrow, I have lost the truest and dearest friend (besides the best of brothers) I ever had, the joy and object of a lifetime.

Believe me yours   sincerely,

LOUISE

The year which followed Prince Leopold's death was a very anxious one for the Queen. The latter part of 1884 saw her actively involved in the fate of Gladstone's Franchise Bill. This, though reasonable in itself, was opposed by the Lords, who insisted that a Redistribution Bill should be brought in simultaneously, fearing that otherwise Gladstone, having enlarged the voters' roll, would proceed to manipulate the result to the advantage of his own party by a subtle scheme of redistribution. Gladstone asked for Tennyson's support in the

Lords, where he had now taken his seat, and Tennyson had replied by urging the Prime Minister to show his hand over redistribution before the Franchise Bill was forced through. The Queen meanwhile, was working on the same lines, though, so far as appears, quite independently – fearing the results for the Conservative party if a head-on clash with the Lords was not prevented. Her efforts were crowned with success, but, by the time the settlement was reached, she and the nation had become seriously apprehensive about the fate of Gordon in the Sudan. By the end of January 1885 the worst had happened – Gordon had lost his life and Khartoum had fallen, entirely, in the Queen's view, owing to the procrastination of the Government.[1]

Tennyson, who had long dreamed of a united and extended Empire under a fully representative Council, leading humanity to 'The Parliament of man, the Federation of the World', was bitterly opposed to Gladstone's Little England policy, though he loved and respected Gladstone, the man. He was therefore fully in sympathy with the Queen's view about Gordon, and it is not surprising that when, in January, 1885, the Princess of Wales wrote, on the coming of age of her eldest son, the Duke of Clarence, saying that she had been in hopes that the Poet Laureate would have been inspired and she herself 'gladdened by a few beautiful lines in honour of the event', Tennyson replied rather grimly,

Madam,

I thank your Royal Highness for your kind letter, and congratulate the young Prince and trust that all Honour and Happiness may attend him thro' life.

[1] Egypt, which was at this time practically administered by Britain, was faced with a revolt in the Sudan under a fanatical leader, the Mahdi. Gladstone's government decided to abandon the Sudan to the rebels, and reluctantly sent General Gordon, who was thought to have great influence with the Sudanese, to negotiate for the release of the Egyptian garrisons who remained trapped in Sudanese Territory. Gordon's influence proved unavailing and he was soon besieged by the Mahdi in Khartoum. All through the summer and autumn Gordon's danger was obvious and the Queen and public opinion urged the government to take action to help him. After much delay an Army was sent under General Wolseley, but it arrived too late, Gordon having been killed by the Mahdi's forces on January 26th, 1885.

To me the paths leading into the future seem somewhat gloomy and (as our Shakespeare says in his *Julius Caesar*) 'crave wary walking,' but then I am an old man in my 76th year, and in spite of my apprehension, the age to come may have its own sunshine both for crown and people. That the Supreme Power may bless you and yours through both worlds is the wish of

Your affectionate servant,

TENNYSON

(Lincoln, A.T.)

Six months later came a request from the Queen which met with an immediate response. This was in connection with the wedding of her youngest daughter, Princess Beatrice, to Prince Henry of Battenberg, one of the four handsome sons, by a morganatic marriage, of Prince Alexander of Hesse. Another of the four brothers was already married to Beatrice's niece, Victoria of Hesse, and a third, Alexander, was prevented only by the opposition of the Czar and Bismarck from marrying Princess Victoria of Prussia, in spite of the support of her mother, the Princess Royal, and her grandmother, Queen Victoria.

When Princess Beatrice's romance came into view, the Queen, in spite of her liking for the Battenbergs, opposed it vigorously, not from any objection to Prince Henry, but simply because she always disliked the marriage of her daughters, and, in this case, could not bear to be parted from her youngest, whose society and support had meant so much to her in recent years and who could have no successor. At last, however, when the young couple agreed that they would live with her after their marriage, she agreed, and the engagement was announced on December 30th, 1884.

The wedding was fixed for July 23rd, 1885, and on July 5th the Queen wrote to Tennyson.

Windsor Castle

July 5th, 1885

You have always been so kind to me, and to my dear Beatrice that I venture to hope you will write 3 or 4 lines (as you did for Princess Frederica) on her marriage.

It is *certainly* a love Match – and I had hoped she would never have married but the loss of her beloved youngest brother made her feel so lonely that she felt the *want* of a younger person of her own age, to lean on.

The young Prince, a soldier and excellent officer, though too young to have been in the German War, is very handsome, universally and deservedly beloved.

His mother was . . . [a piece is here torn out], his father – Alexander of Hesse is Uncle to my Son-in-law the Grand-duke of Hesse – the widower of dear Alice.

Prince Henry is brother to Prince Louis of Battenberg who married Victoria of Hesse, dear Alice's eldest child, and is in our Navy, and to the Prince of Bulgaria – They are – [piece torn away]. – dear Beatrice will live with me as heretofore, without which I *never* could have *allowed* the marriage, nor could she ever have thought of it as she never would have left me. – I have written all this to you, thinking you might kindly like to know about it.

You know how alone I am and feel for me! And since I saw you – I lost my dear son Leopold.

Hoping you are well,

> Ever
> Yours truly,
>
> V.R.I.

Tennyson replied with an alacrity in marked contrast to his grim response to the Princess of Wales's request, and his poem (afterwards published in *Tiresias and Other Poems*, Macmillan, 1885) tactfully hinted at the dilemma in which the Queen had found herself, and its happy solution.

I am honoured by your Majesty's most gracious letter and if I am fortunate enough to write what your Majesty would have me write and as your Majesty would have it written, I shall have true pleasure in having written.

The account of the young Prince is very interesting and Your Majesty may well believe that in him another will be added to Your 'Army of Heroes'.

England, whose heart has rarely, if ever, beaten more warmly for her soldiers, nor with better cause than now, will rejoice that the Princess, whom she has loved as the devoted daughter has every prospect of being the happy wife of a soldier Prince

and of bringing a new solace to the life which year by year
becomes more precious to the whole Empire.

(Lincoln, E.T. and H.T.)

TO H.R.H. PRINCESS BEATRICE

Two Suns of Love make day of human life,
Which else with all its pains, and griefs, and deaths,
Were utter darkness – one, the Sun of dawn
That brightens thro' the Mother's tender eyes,
And warms the child's awakening world – and one
The later-rising Sun of spousal Love,
Which from her household orbit draws the child
To move in other spheres. The Mother weeps
At that white funeral of the single life,
Her maiden daughter's marriage; and her tears
Are half of pleasure, half of pain – the child
Is happy – ev'n in leaving her! but Thou
True daughter, whose all-faithful filial eyes
Have seen the loneliness of earthly thrones,
Wilt neither quit the widow'd Crown nor let
This later light of Love have risen in vain,
But moving thro' the Mother's home, between
The two that love thee, lead a summer life,
Sway'd by each Love, and swaying to each Love,
Like some conjectured planet in mid heaven
Between two Suns, and drawing down from both
The light and genial warmth of double day.

Although it is said that the Princess was rather distressed by
the reference to the 'white funeral', the lines greatly pleased
the Queen, as is shown by her letter of July 12th, the third letter
in the remarkable exchange of correspondence which followed.

First comes the Queen's reply to Tennyson's letter just
quoted, which apparently did not include the poem. By the
time this letter was written Gladstone's government had been
beaten over its Budget, and Lord Salisbury had become Prime
Minister.

Windsor Castle
July 8th, 1885

I am so grateful and touched by your kind letter.
It would give me the greatest of pleasures if you would come

over for the Wedding in our Village Church – but I *fear* you will not do that! But pray come and see me when all is quiet again.

You will understand that Prince Henry though an excellent Soldier has never been in the Field as he was too young, the last German War being fifteen years ago and he is only 26½.

You may also like to know that she will be followed by her *10* nieces, as Bridesmaids, viz: my eldest son's *3* girls, Louise, Victoria and Maud of Wales – dear Alice's *2* motherless girls Irene and Alice of Hesse – Princess Christian's *2* Victoria & Louise of Holstein and my son Alfred's *3* – Marie, Victoria and Alexandra Marie of Edinburgh.

> I am
> Yours
> Very Truly
> V.R.I.

P.S. I have suffered very much during the last 6 or 7 months on account of the fatal mistakes made by the late Government in Egypt and the Sudan – when they interfered and checked and stopped what was necessary and were always too late – thereby being the cause of the death of that noble Hero Gordon (whose abandonment is an eternal blot on our crown, though *not* on the *Nation!*)

The Tennyson Research Centre has two versions of a reply to the Queen's letter, one, dated July 9th, 1885, in Emily Tennyson's handwriting, one dated July 10th, 1885, in Princess Louise's hand.

Both the versions are printed below. In the absence of the letter actually sent, which has unfortunately disappeared, it is impossible to be sure of the exact terms of Tennyson's reply It seems probable that the version copied by Princess Louise was actually used, though the copy may not be entirely accurate.

> *July 9th*, 1885

Your Majesty is most gracious but I think that blind as I am, I am best away from the Wedding, and I must ask to be excused.

It cannot fail to be a touching and beautiful sight.

Should the poem which I send be approved of by Your

Majesty and the Princess, I will have some copies printed for
your Majesty.

Very often in the sorrowful period through which we have
passed, we have thought of what Your Majesty must have
suffered.

It cheers one that the present Prime Minister speaks only
of the interest of the Empire, leaving, at all events in abeyance,
the fatal cry of party, and the consequent flattery of the
people.

The dying exhortation of La Place to an Englishman, 'never
tamper with your glorious constitution', is for ever sounding
in my heart.

Well indeed would it have been for us had we heeded the
warning!

We should have been spared all these humiliating bewilder-
ments and most of the other sore evils which have saddened
us had we done so.

(Lincoln, E.T.)

July 10th, 1885

Your Majesty is most gracious but I think that blind as I
am and daily I fear growing blinder, I am best away from the
Wedding – and I would pray to be excused except that Your
Majesty had kindly anticipated my excuse for absence from
a ceremony which cannot fail to be beautiful and touching.

Should the Poem which I send be approved by Your Majesty
and the Princess shall I have some copies printed?

Very often in the sorrowful period thro' which we have
passed we have thought of what the Queen must have
suffered.

It cheers me that the Present Prime Minister speaks only of
the interests of the Empire, leaving, at all events in abeyance
the fatal cry of Party.

Change must needs come in all human things, but I wish that
Statesmen would oftener remember the saying of Bacon, 'Man
in innovating should imitate the work of time, which innovateth
slowly but surely' (or some such words). We might then have
such stability in our policy as is possible to our poor human
nature.

I fully sympathise with yr Majesty's feelings for our great
simple soldier hero Gordon and I rejoice that the Mansion
House Committee have adopted as the National Memorial the

Scheme proposed by myself and my son which had its origin in a conversation with Gordon.[1]

> Believe me
> Your Majesty's loyal & affectionate servant
> T. (Lincoln, Princess Louise)

The Queen's reply to this made the rather startling suggestion that her Poet Laureate should endeavour to induce Gladstone to retire from Politics. It is noteworthy that to this letter she, for the first time, signs herself 'yours affectionately'.

> *Osborne*
> *July* 12*th,* 1885

How *can* I sufficiently thank you for those exquisite touching, beautiful lines which I read to my beloved Child, who was equally delighted with them and with the beautiful thoughts they contain. I know not if you may not require the original Poem for the printing which we much desire and therefore return it. But beg to have it back again as I shall value it so much in your own hand. –

We should particularly wish to have copies of the Poem.

Can you not have some influence with Mr Gladstone in preventing his making another round of agitation in the autumn – a repetition of the Midlothian Campaign in 80 – which did such incalculable harm, and standing again in the New Parliament. Ever since he took office in 80 he said he wished soon to retire and quite lately repeated & now the contrary.

Radicals wish to push him on at 75½ to do what will ruin his reputation more than this last Government has already done.

It is as much for his own reputation as for the good of the Country that I urge this on all who are his friends.

> Ever
> Yours
> affecty.
>
> V.R.I.

I hope you will read our simple soldier hero's diary. It is intensely interesting but heartrending and [illegible] more brave men – and poor wild fanatics.

But men fought never better or endured more – or deserved more praise at their country's and Sovereign's hands. But

---

[1] The foundation of 'The Gordon Boys' Home'.

your friend the former Prime Minister never gave them any – and has much to answer for. No warnings of mine or of those who knew what was necessary were heeded.

In his reply of 20th July, 1885, Tennyson undertakes, with some misgivings, the Queen's very embarrassing request.

We print this reply from a copy made by Princess Louise at the Queen's request in 1895 and sent to Hallam Lord Tennyson in connection with his *Memoir* of the poet, where, however, it does not appear. The Tennyson Research Centre has a slightly differing draft in the poet's handwriting which we print as a footnote.[1]

July 20, 1885

Madam,
   I have sent Your Majesty one hundred copies of the Poem printed. I am glad your Princess approves it for I who enter my 77th year on the 8th August [*sic*] might well give in to the fear that the flower of Poetry was faded or fading in me but for Your Majesty's and the Royal bride's approval to whom the old Poet sends his blessing and his wish 'Queen's weather' on the 23rd. Would indeed that any word of mine could hinder a

[1]
         Farringford,
         Freshwater,
         Isle of Wight
         20th July 1885
    (date in Hallam Tennyson's hand)

Madam,
   I have sent Your Majesty one hundred copies of the poem printed.
   I am glad that Your Majesty & your dear Princess approve it, for I who enter on the 6th August [Prince Albert's birthday*] my 77th year might well give in to the fear that the flower of Poetry was faded or fading in me, but for your Majesty's and the Royal Bride's approval.
   The old Poet sends his blessing to her.
   Would indeed that any word of mine could hinder a second Midlothian campaign: but Mr Gladstone differs in so many of his political views from myself that whatever I say on these subjects would have I fear no weight with him – however I can but try, in being
      Your Majesty's
      loyally & affty.
      TENNYSON
        (Lincoln, A.T.)

---

* Prince Albert's birthday was August 26th, 1819. Perhaps Princess Louise omitted the reference in her copy of Tennyson's letter because of the mistake.

second Midlothian Campaign: but Mr Gladstone differs in so many of his political views from myself that whatever I might say on these subjects would have I fear little or no weight with him.

However, I can but try, being your Majesty's

loyal and devoted servant

T.

Eighteen days later the Queen writes to congratulate the poet on his 76th birthday, a very intimate and affectionate letter, but with a sting in the tail.

Osborne
August 7th, 1885

I was not unmindful of yesterday's Anniversary and would wish to offer my warm good wishes on the return of your natal day.

It was also my son Alfred's and my Son-in-Law Lorne's birthday and there was always a gathering at Osborne Cottage of my children, grandchildren and Relations and as I gazed on the happy young couple and on my 2 sons, Alfred and Arthur and their 'bonnie bairns' I could not but feel sad – in thinking that their hour of trial might come and earnestly prayed God would spare my sweet Beatrice and the Husband she so truly loves and confides in – for long long to each other!

Till 61 no real inroad of any kind had been made in our *own* circle and how heavy has God's Hand been since then on me!!

Mother, Husband, Children, truest friends all have been taken from me and yet I must 'still endure' and I shall try to do so! – Your beautiful lines have been greatly admired.

I wish you could have *seen* the Wedding for everyone says it was the prettiest they had ever seen.

The simple pretty little village church all decorated with flowers, the sweet young Bride, the handsome young Husband, the 10 Bridesmaids 6 of whom quite children with flowing fair hair, the brilliant sunshine and the blue sea all made up pictures not to be forgotten.

Believe me always
Yours affectionately,

V.R.I.

Have you heard from Mr Gladstone?
The Lord Tennyson.

By this time Tennyson had already spoken to Gladstone with the result which he anticipated.

Three versions of his reply exist, one written by Princess Louise, made presumably in 1895, one by Hallam Tennyson and one by Emily Tennyson. The differences are insignificant, except that Princess Louise, for obvious reasons, omits the reference to Gladstone. The version printed below, represents, we believe, the letter as actually sent.

Aldworth
August 9th, 1885

Madam,

Tho' feasts and flowers seem to me only properly to belong to the birthdays of the young, and though I myself always pass my own over in silence, yet believe me most thoroughly grateful for your Majesty's gracious and kindly congratulations.

As to the sufferings of this momentary life, we can but trust that in some after state, when we see clearer, we shall thank the Supreme Power for having made us, through *them* higher and greater Beings.

Still it surely cannot be unlawful to pray that our children and our children's children may pass through smoother waters to the other shore.

The wedding must have been beautiful. The Peace of Heaven seemed in the day.

Mr Gladstone goes no further than to say he will not if he can help it. Should I hear anything more decisive, I will, if your Majesty will allow me, write again.

Your Majesty's affectionate subject
TENNYSON

In the spring of 1886 a severe blow struck the poet. His second son, Lionel, who had just begun a promising career at the India Office, caught jungle fever on a visit to the Viceroy Lord Dufferin, and died on the way home on April 20th, leaving a young wife, a niece of Lady Augusta Bruce, and three small children.

Four days before the Queen had written:

Osborne
April 16th, 1886

I cannot refrain from writing to express my deep concern

and true sympathy with you and Lady Tennyson who I know must be spared as much anxiety as possible at the present moment when you are in such trouble about your dear Son.

I am indeed grieved beyond measure for you and your dear wife, and for poor little Eleanor whom I have known from her earliest childhood.

God grant that you may yet get better news!

Beatrice shares my feelings having known Eleanor so well.

I cannot in this letter allude to Politics but I know what your feelings must be!

> Believe me always
> Yours Truly,
>
> v.r.i.

The Queen's reference to Politics at the end of her letter was no doubt caused by the dispute then raging over the Home Rule Bill, which Gladstone, who had come back to power at the beginning of the year, had introduced in the House of Commons on April 8th. Tennyson evidently prepared two alternative drafts of a reply to this letter (both at Lincoln). One he discarded, probably thinking it unsuitable to the occasion.

We print the other draft which exists at Lincoln in Tennyson's own hand. There is also at Lincoln an almost identical copy in Emily's hand dated April 1886. Lincoln also has a copy in Princess Louise's hand, no doubt made from the letter actually sent, and dated 'August 18, 1886'. We have not used this copy as it is obviously inaccurate, both in the date (August for April) and in one or two less important details.

> *Farringford,*
> *Freshwater,*
> *Isle of Wight*

Madam,

I beg to offer to Your Majesty the assurance of my own and my wife's heartfelt gratitude for Your Majesty's most welcome letter of sympathy with us, and may I also add our sense of the kindness of H.R.H. Princess Beatrice in thinking of us.

Our last telegram was from Colombo, 'no improvement', but in this pause, as it were, between life and death – since Your Majesty touches upon the disastrous policy of the day – I may say, that I wish I may be in my own grave beyond sight and hearing when an English army fires upon the Loyalists of Ulster.

> Believe me always your Majesty's
> Loyal and affectionate subject
> TENNYSON
> (Lincoln, A.T.)

The exceedingly interesting discarded draft is as follows:

I beg to offer to Your Majesty the assurance of my own and my wife's heartfelt gratitude for your Majesty's most gracious letter of sympathy with us and ours and may I also add our sense of the kindness of H.R.H. Princess Beatrice in thinking of us.

We can have no further news we believe before Wednesday or Thursday but even in this most sad and solemn pause in our lives we feel deeply the state of public affairs.

Let it not be thought possible that England should yield up at the bidding of a band of robbers and assassins and those deluded by them all that is dearest to a nation.

We can never abandon the loyal Irish, never submit to give up any under Your Majesty's rule, whether loyal or disloyal to their ruin and our shame.

Differences of race should be a source of strength and not of weakness to a Kingdom because of the diversities of gifts which it brings.

At all events all kindreds of men on the face of the earth are under one moral law and all just human laws are founded on this. Where then is the plea for any special laws for Ireland – Customs there may be and let them be admitted. If only this humiliating crisis cause conviction that the time for govern-ment by party has past, I think that your Majesty and your subjects will have reason to be thankful that we have had to pass through it.

Men from natural tendencies will inevitably fall into some-thing of party but let it be no longer a point of honour to adhere to a party. This point of honour being so easily overstrained.

> (Lincoln, A.T.)

Two letters from the Queen written after hearing of Lionel's death survive. The first she evidently sent by special messenger. The second was addressed to Hallam.

Osborne
April 25th, 1886

I wish I could express in words how *deeply* and truly I feel for you in this hour of heavy affliction!

You, who have written such words of comfort for others will, I feel sure, feel the comfort of them again in yourself.

But it is *terrible* to lose one's grown up children, when one is no longer young oneself – and to see, as I have done – and you will do now – the sore stricken young widow of one's beloved son!

I will not weary you or intrude on your grief, by words of consolation, which in fact *can* offer none. But I say from the depth of a heart which has suffered cruelly – and lost almost all it cared for and loved best – I *feel* for you. I know what you and your dear wife are suffering, and I pray God to support you.

Pray let your son Hallam write me a few words by the messenger who takes this over, and say how you and Lady Tennyson are. –

My dear Beatrice grieves deeply for her former playmate poor dear Eleanor, and is very anxious to hear how she is.

Ever
Yours afftely,

v.r.i.

I am very grateful for your kind letter.

The Queen's letter to Hallam Tennyson was as follows:

Osborne
April 26th, 1886

The Queen is very thankful to Mr Tennyson for his kind sad letter and for the Enclosure from Lord Dufferin.

It is terribly sad.

She trusts his dear Mother will be mercifully supported and that fresh news will soon be received from poor Eleanor and that the 1st meeting will not be too trying for her and for Lord and Lady Tennyson.

The Queen feels deeply for Mr Tennyson to whom the loss of this only Brother must be a heavy blow, and lasting sorrow.

All through these weeks of intense anxiety about his son Tennyson had, at the special request of the Prince of Wales, been working on an ode to be sung at the opening by the

Queen, on May 4th, 1886, of the Indian and Colonial Exhibition. He carried this commission out faithfully in spite of his personal anxiety and grief, making his ode an expression of the romantic Imperialism which the Queen so passionately shared (see *Works*, pp. 577–8).

The last lines of the poem are characteristic.

> *. . . Sharers of our glorious past,*
> *Brothers, must we part at last?*
> *Shall we not thro' good and ill*
> *Cleave to one another still?*
> *Britain's myriad voices call,*
> *'Sons be welded each and all,*
> *Into one imperial whole,*
> *One with Britain, heart and soul,*
> *One life, one flag, one fleet, one Throne!'*
> *Britons, hold your own!*

It was perhaps some consolation to read in the *Times* report of the opening ceremony that the twelve thousand people present 'were deeply moved remembering his sorrow'.

But the depression clung to him and in December of this year (1886) he issued his most pessimistic poem, 'Locksley Hall Sixty Years After,' in which he expressed with extraordinary passion his disappointment at the moral and political progress achieved since the publication of the first 'Locksley Hall' nearly fifty years before.

Gladstone was so much disturbed by this outburst that in the issue of the *Nineteenth Century* for January 1887 he took up the challenge with an elaborately deferential article in which he gave an impressive catalogue of the reforms adopted by Parliament since 1842, concluding with a reference to the forthcoming celebration of the fiftieth year of Victoria's reign. 'Justice does not require, nay rather she forbids, that the Jubilee of the Queen be marred by tragic notes.'

When Gladstone's article appeared Tennyson was already hard at work on his Jubilee ode (ultimately published in *Macmillans Magazine* for April 1887). As usual, when he had an official job to tackle, he made full use of his rhythmic and verbal virtuosity to compensate for the inevitable lack of authentic inspiration, alternating three-line addresses to the Queen in bouncing trochaics, with longer exhortations to her subjects based on the exhilarating metre of his favourite Latin poet Catullus's 'Epithalamium on the marriage of Jurina and Manlius.' But in the eleventh section the tone of the trochaics changed (it is said, with the Queen's express approval) to a note which, if not actually tragic, was at least one of apprehensive warning.

> *. . . Are there thunders moaning in the distance?*
> *Are there spectres moving in the darkness?*
> *Trust the Hand of Light will lead her people,*
> *Till the thunders pass, the spectres vanish,*
> *And the Light is Victor, and the darkness*
> *Dawns into the Jubilee of the Ages.*

The Queen was delighted with the ode which Tennyson sent her early in March, at a time when she was in considerable anxiety and distress on behalf of Alexander, second of the handsome and distinguished Battenberg brothers, and Princess Beatrice's brother-in-law. In 1879, after the Treaty of Berlin, Alexander, when only twenty-two years old, had, at the instance of the Czar, been elected Prince of Bulgaria. After eight uneasy years marked by some brilliant achievements, including a striking victory over the invading Serbians at Slivinitza in November 1885, he had found himself compelled to abdicate by the hostility of the Czar and Bismarck, who disapproved of the advance under his rule of Bulgarian nationalism.

> *Windsor Castle*
> *March 6th, 1887*

I am most grateful for your kind letter enclosing the beautiful Ode you have written for my Jubilee. Beatrice deeply regrets having lost the opportunity of hearing you read it, and of not having had the pleasure of paying you a visit with her Husband. But the very cold north east wind would have made a long drive rather trying. They hope to have the pleasure of visiting you another time.

The news of the serious illness of their heroic and distin-

The letter sent to Alfred Tennyson by the Queen with a copy of her More Leaves from a Journal in the Highlands (see page 110)

Alfred Tennyson in 1869, photographed by Julia Margaret Cameron

guished Brother Prince Alexander only reached us just before
we left Osborne, and the fact of his having caught the smallpox
only came to our knowledge a few days later – He is now happily
convalescent – but it does seem hard indeed, after all the
dangers and trials he has gone through, to have had this
terrible illness *now*. It would give me much pleasure to hear your
Ode performed and I hope some arrangement may be made to
enable this to be done. – The unusual feeling of loyalty and
affection displayed on this occasion is very gratifying to me; –
but your kind and sympathising heart will understand me
when I say how much sorrow there is mingled in it – when I feel
that the dear, great Husband to whom I and the Country owe
so much, and who could have entered into it all so warmly
cannot be by my side; and that two dear gifted Children as
well as some very dear friends who would have so truly rejoiced
to see this day will also be missing – I shall feel so *alone*. Your
blessing is very precious to me and I thank you from my heart
for it. –

Trusting that Lady Tennyson and Eleanor are pretty well,
believe me,

Yours affectionately,

v.r. & i.

As you speak with interest of dear Prince Alexander I think
that you might be interested in reading these letters written
directly after the dreadful revolution at Sofia, by his eldest
brother Prince Louis of Battenberg who married my Gd.
daughter – dear Pss. Alice's eldest daughter, as well as one of
Prince Alexander's to me explaining the cause of his inability
to remain.

Their perusal will fill you with indignation, I am sure. I fear
the copies are rather soiled for they have been sent to several
people to read – please return them at your leisure.

The name 'Sandro' is taken from Allessandro, and is the
name by which Pce Alexander is always called by his family and
relations. 'Franzjos' is an abbreviation of Francis Joseph and
is the name by which the youngest brother who shared his
elder brother's dangers in war on this last terrible occasion,
was familiarly called.

March 6, 1887.   v.r.i.

Tennyson's reply showed that he sympathised as fully as the
Queen herself with the misfortunes of the handsome romantic

'Sandro' who retired to Graz where he died on October 23rd, 1893, a forlorn and frustrated young man of thirty-six.

March 12*th,* 1887

Madam,

I am grateful for Your Majesty's most kind letter and for the privilege of reading the deeply interesting communications from Prince Alexander and Prince Louis.

Rarely indeed have the tragic scenes of perfidy, cruelty, baseness which they so touchingly relate been equalled.

They make one ashamed of one's kind.

Poor Alexander the Pr., or rather poor Alexander the Czar, who seems to have behaved so dishonourably that his name on the page of true History will look as blurred, as that other's will be bright – a man of noble and self-sacrificing nature. I say true History, for what we call History is too often no truer than the babble of a village gossip.

I do indeed feel how the sense of loneliness may oppress Y.M. in the midst of these loud rejoicings.

'Ihr Beifall selbst macht meinem Herzen bang', as Goethe says in his preface to Faust. The multitude are loud, but *They* are silent. Yet if the dead, as I have often felt, tho' silent, be more living than the living – and linger for a while about the planet in which their earth life was passed – then they, while we are lamenting that they are not at our side, may still be with us, and the husband the daughter and the son lost by Yr M. may rejoice when the people shout the name of their Queen.

(Lincoln, Princess Louise)

The ode was set to music by Charles Villiers Stanford, the friend of Hallam and Lionel Tennyson, whom Tennyson had brought into prominence by securing for him the commission to compose the incidental music to his drama *Queen Mary* in 1876. As Tennyson, who was now in his seventy-eighth year, did not feel able to attend the performance the Queen was careful to inform him of its success.

Windsor Castle
May 14*th,* 1887

I am anxious to tell you that your beautiful Ode was performed at Buckingham Palace on the 11th, with a full Orchestra, Solo, Gala, and choruses and conducted by Mr Stanford himself.

We greatly admired the music which was very descriptive and well adapted to the words – and it was extremely well executed. I wish you could have heard it.

We have just returned from opening the People's Palace. There was an enormous crowd everywhere and much enthusiasm and loyalty.

I must thank you for your last kind letter and hope that you are well, as also Lady Tennyson and your family.

Believe me always
Yours affectionately
V.R.I.

Tennyson's letter to Princess Beatrice of February 15th, 1888, following a visit to Farringford by the Princess, Prince Henry of Battenberg and Sir Henry Ponsonby, agreeably concludes the story of the Jubilee Ode.

February 15th, 1888
Farringford
Freshwater
Isle of Wight

Madam,

I did not know till after Your Royal Highness had left us yesterday when I opened the parcel, that the Memorial of the Jubilee Year was the photograph of the Queen.

If I did not express my loyal thanks to Your Royal Highness sufficiently by word of mouth for the kind and gracious gift allow me to write them here.

Yesterday's visit will always be a pleasant memory to me and I trust your Royal Highness has already forgiven me for introducing you to such low company as my old 'Spinster and her Cats'.[1]

With our dutiful remembrances
I am
Your Royal Highness's
faithful servant

TENNYSON
(Lincoln, E.T. and H.T.)

[1] 'The Spinster's Sweet-Arts', one of Tennyson's famous poems in the Lincolnshire dialect, which he particularly enjoyed reading aloud, published in *Tiresias and other Poems* (Macmillan, 1885).

In the winter of 1888–9 Tennyson had a severe attack of rheumatic gout from which his doctors did not expect him to recover. However, his great strength and will-power pulled him through and his eightieth birthday on August 6th, 1889, was an occasion of national rejoicing, letters and telegrams pouring in from all over the world. The Queen, in spite of many absorbing engagements, did not forget the day.

Osborne
August 9th, 1889

Though 3 days late, I hope I may still offer my best wishes for your 80th birthday and my hope that many more anniversaries may follow.

My time has been so much taken up by my Grandson, the Emperor of Germany's visit that I have hardly been able to write, but my thoughts were with you, on a day which is dear to me from being the birthday of my second Son and Son-in-Law Ld Lorne.

My grandson the Emperor of Germany's visit went off very well and much cordiality between the two Countries was shown on both sides.

Trusting that you are now quite recovered from your long illness.

believe me always
Yours
affly.

v.r.i.

Pray remember me to Lady Tennyson.

Tennyson's reply was prophetic.

Aldworth
Haslemere
August 89

Madam,

Your Majesty has given yet another proof of that universal kindness which has rejoiced so many hearts by remembering your old Poet's birthday and making time to tell him so in the midst of almost overwhelming work.

That the Emperor's visit has passed off so well must be a source of thankfulness not only to Your Majesty but to the two Nations, nations too closely allied by the subtle sympathy of kindred not to be either true brothers or deadly foes.

As brothers what might they not do for the world!

May those so near and dear to Your Majesty as son and son-in-law find every 6th of August happier and happier to themselves in the consciousness of good achieved.

I have had nine months of the most painful and depressing illness. My doctors say that such an attack of rheumatic gout at my age very frequently is fatal. I am much better now, but probably I shall never be quite the same man again though always the same I trust in my devotion to the Queen and my loyalty to Her Throne of England.

TENNYSON

My wife is most grateful for Your Majesty's most gracious remembrance.

> (Lincoln, E.T. and copy by Princess Louise omitting PS.)

Tennyson had felt unable to accept a request from the Prince of Wales in May 1889 that he would compose an ode for the laying of the foundation stone of the Imperial Institute by the Queen. Perhaps she had arranged for the Prince to write, instead of herself, in order that the poet might be able to refuse with less embarrassment if he felt unable to undertake a rather onerous task so soon after his serious illness.

Early in 1890 came an appeal from Princess Beatrice which, as his reply shows, he found much more congenial.

Dear Lord Tennyson,

It is with some diffidence I address you these lines to ask a favour of you in mine and my eldest sister's name.

Next Monday is the 50th anniversary of our Parents' wedding, and her children are going to give Mama a prayer book in an antique cover. My Sister was anxious that a few appropriate words in verse should be placed at the beginning and our first thought was to ask you. Mama being such a great admirer of all you write, any words of yours on this momentous anniversary would greatly enhance the value of the book. My only fear is, you may think we are asking too much of you.

I was glad to hear you were well, when I inquired after you, on passing Farringford this afternoon,

and believe me dear Ld Tennyson

Osborne   Yours truly
February 3, 1890   BEATRICE
                                          (Lincoln, E.T.)

Tennyson's reply which only survives in a copy on Osborne notepaper, dated February 10th, 1890, must have been written earlier, for Princess Beatrice's answer is dated from Osborne on February 7th. February 10th was in fact the date of the presentation.

Madam,
The old man of 80 has done what he could in compliance with your Royal Highness's request. The term 'Golden Wedding' signifies that Husband and Wife have lived together for 50 years, but since we believe that *He* is still living, let 'Golden' stand –

(signed) TENNYSON

Remembering Him who waits thee far away,
And with thee, Mother, taught us first to pray,
Accept on this your golden bridal-day
The Book of Prayer.

TENNYSON
(Royal Archives, Windsor, Add. A. 15/5418)

Osborne
February, 7th, 1890

Dear Lord Tennyson,
It is most kind of you to have so soon responded to my request, and I am sure my Brothers & Sisters will admire as much as I do, the beautiful words you have written.
Thanking you once more most sincerely for all the trouble you have taken, which I know will be much appreciated by Mama.

Believe me
Yours truly,
BEATRICE

The Queen was so pleased with Tennyson's ready response to the Princess's request and the lines which resulted from it, that on the very day of the presentation she sent a special messenger with a letter of thanks and photographs of some *Tableaux vivants* at Osborne to which Hallam had been invited. Tennyson's telegram has not been found.

Osborne
February 10, 1890

How kind it is of you to have written those beautiful lines and to have sent the telegram for this ever dear day, which I will never allow to be considered a sad day. The reflected light of the sun which has set still remains! It is full of pathos – but also full of joyful gratitude and He who has left me nearly 29 years ago – surely blesses me still!

Your son, whose acquaintance I was much pleased to make, was desirous of getting the Photographs of our Tableaux which he saw – and I send a set today for your acceptance, hoping you may be interested by them.

I hope that you are well and that I may some day see you again.

Asking you to remember me kindly to Lady Tennyson and your Son, believe me always,

Yours
affectionately,
VICTORIA R.I.

Tennyson's acknowledgment, which only survives in a copy at Lincoln by Princess Louise, may well have been taken back by Queen's messenger.

February, 10, 1890

Madam,

I am glad that your Majesty did not consider my lines out of harmony with the sacred day. No words could more entirely express the feelings which of right belong to it than Your Majesty's.

The photographs of the Tableaux are most interesting. They will, I need not say, ever be highly prized, both for the Giver's sake and as a memorial of the pleasant days my son spent at Osborne when his Queen was so gracious and kind to him.

My wife and son send their most loyal duty.

I am ever yr. Majesty's grateful and affect. servant,

TENNYSON
(Lincoln, Princess Louise)

A year later Hallam was again invited to a showing of *Tableaux Vivants* at Osborne, this time scenes from 'Lancelot and Elaine' were included.

Once more the Queen sent photographs.

Osborne
February, 9th, 1891

I venture to send you two photographs of the Tableaux Vivants of 'Elaine' ,which your Son will have told you of – and which I hope you will like.

Of course the want of colour prevents the effect being as fine as it was but I think they are very good.

Our Stage is very small so that it cramps large groups.

Our new room will be finished next year when I hope we may be able to represent larger tableaux or at least to bring in more people without crowding.

Hoping that you and Lady Tennyson are well.

Believe me ever,
Yours affectionately,
VICTORIA R.I.

Tennyson's reply of February 11th is one of the few letters in his hand preserved at Windsor.

Farringford
February, 11th, 1891

Madam,

I am very grateful for Your Majesty's kind letter, and for the photographs of the Tableaux.

That of Elaine in the boat seems beautiful, and Arthur's Court with the splendid colouring and old armour must have been very effective.

May I be allowed to add how much my son and his wife felt the kindness of the reception at Osborne and how much they enjoyed the plays. I am glad to hear from them that Your Majesty is looking so well.

With the loyal devotion of my wife and myself.

I am
Your Majesty's ever affectionate servant
TENNYSON
(Royal Archives, Windsor L.21/1)

On August 6th of this year, 1891, Tennyson reached his eighty-second birthday, which was marked by exchanges of telegrams both with the Queen and the Prince and Princess of Wales.

On January 14th, 1892, the Duke of Clarence, eldest son of

the Prince of Wales, died suddenly, within six weeks of the
announcement of his engagement to Princess Mary of Teck
(afterwards Queen Mary, wife of King George V). Tennyson
was deeply shocked by this event. Remembering that he had
not felt inspired to celebrate in verse the young man's coming
of age, he immediately, though feeling far from well at the
time, set about a poem of consolation for the bereaved family.
The poem was sent to the Queen some days before the end of
the month (there is evidently a mistake in the dating of his
letter to her of January 30th).

Farringford
January, 30th, 1892

Madam,

I venture to write but I do not know how to express
the profound sympathy of myself and my family with the
great sorrow which has befallen Your Majesty and your
children.

I know that Your Majesty has a perfect trust in the Love
and Wisdom which order the circumstances of our life and in
this alone is there comfort.

TENNYSON
(Lincoln E.T. 2 copies)

It is not clear whether the poem was sent with this letter.

'The Death of the Duke of Clarence and Avondale'
To the Mourners

The bridal garland falls upon the bier,
The shadow of a crown, that o'er him hung,
Has vanish'd in the shadow cast by Death.
So princely, tender, truthful, reverent, pure –
Mourn! That a world-wide Empire mourns with you,
That all the Thrones are clouded by your loss,
Were slender solace. Yet be comforted;
For if this earth be ruled by Perfect Love,
Then, after his brief range of blameless days,
The toll of funeral in an Angel ear
Sounds happier than the merriest marriage-bell.
The face of Death is toward the Sun of Life,
His shadow darkens earth: his truer name

Is 'Onward,' no discordance in the roll
And march of that Eternal Harmony
Whereto the worlds beat time, tho' faintly heard
Until the great Hereafter. Mourn in hope!

The letters from the Queen, The Prince of Wales and Lord Lorne, the Queen's son-in-law, show how deeply the poem was appreciated. It is curious that the Queen here returns to the third person formula –

Osborne
January, 28th, 1892

The Queen is very deeply touched by the beautiful lines Lord Tennyson has so kindly written and sent on this Terrible Tragedy – which is a real misfortune.

She thanks him warmly for writing and sending them. They are most affecting. But was there ever a more terrible contrast?

A wedding with bright hopes turned into a funeral in the very chapel where the former was to have taken place.

The Queen hopes that Lord Tennyson is well in the midst of so much illness everywhere.

She keeps well but she is deeply grieved by the loss of her dearly loved Grandson.

From the Marquess of Lorne.

My dear Lord Tennyson,

The Queen was very much touched and very much pleased with what you wrote and sent to her.

She is specially anxious that you should not think that the delay that has arisen in her acknowledgement has been owing to any want of feeling; but it has come through want of time for since her loss she has been overwhelmed with work. As soon as the touching lines came she spoke with tears in her eyes of their beauty, and I know that she felt much your goodness in sending them, and that they were really a comfort to her.

Believe me, dear Lord Tennyson,

Yours very truly,

LORNE

Osborne, January, 28, 1892

From the Prince of Wales.

Osborne
February, 2nd, 1892

My dear Lord Tennyson,
  The beautiful Poem dedicated to the beloved son we have lost
has deeply touched our hearts, but what has greatly enhanced
its value in our eyes is that you have sent a copy of it to the
Princess and myself written in your hand.
  You may be assured that we shall always greatly prize it and
that the verses emanating from so distinguished a pen will ever
remain a solace for us in our grief.
  Believe me,

Very sincerely Yours
ALBERT EDWARD

Tennyson was already in poor health when he undertook the
lines on the Duke of Clarence. There seems to be no doubt that
the effort and the stress of feeling started a decline. All through
the summer his condition slowly deteriorated. At the beginning
of September the position became serious. In the early hours of
October 6th he died, having retained consciousness and some
degree of mental power until a few hours before the end, so
that he was able to realise and appreciate the coming of a
telegram which the Queen sent from Balmoral at about 4 on
the afternoon of the 5th.

I cannot say how distressed I am to hear of the alarming
state of your dear Honoured father. How is your mother.

V.R.I.

To this Hallam replied before 6.

We feel very deeply Your Majesty's goodness to him and to
all of us. He is still passing away peacefully. My mother is
crushed but brave and thankful that he does not suffer.

(Royal Archives, Windsor, R.44/1)

At 9.30 next morning Hallam telegraphed news of the end.

My father passed away very peacefully about 1.30 this morning. During his illness his gratitude to our three selves, Dr
Dabbs and his nurse was most touching. Sir Andrew Clark

kindly came from Christchurch yesterday. My Father's last conscious effort was to call 'Hallam' and whisper to my Mother, 'God bless you my joy,' As he awaited death the full moon poured through the oriel window on his grand face and on his hand clasping the Shakespeare which he had been reading. Outside the window was the great landscape that he could see from where he lay flooded with glory. It was the noblest imaginable picture of the passing of King Arthur.

HALLAM TENNYSON

(Royal Archives, Windsor, R.44/1A)

From this point the correspondence can be left to tell its own story.

From the Queen's diary.

October 6, 1892

A fine morning – I heard that dear old Ld Tennyson had breathed his last, a great national loss. He was a great poet, and his ideas were ever grand, noble, elevating. He was very loyal and always very kind and sympathising to me, quite remarkably so. What beautiful lines he wrote to me for my darling Albert, and for my children and Eddy. He died with his hand on his Shakespeare, and the moon shining full into the window, and over him. A worthy end to such a remarkable man.

From Balgorrie   *6th October*, 1892
To the Queen, Balmoral.   1.5 p.m.
                                                          1.25 p.m.
Dear old Lord Tennyson's death so sad. Finer today.

LOUISE

(Royal Archives, Windsor, R.44/1B)

O.H.M.S.   *October 6*, 1892
From Balmoral – 11.45 – Noon.
To Hon. Hallam Tennyson, Haslemere.

Most truly deeply grieved that the great poet and kind friend has left this world. He was ever so kind to me and so full of sympathy. Feel so deeply for your dear mother and yourself his devoted son.

V.R.I.

Balmoral Castle
October, 6th, 1892

The Queen thanks Mr Tennyson again for his very touching Telegram describing the passing away of his beloved Father, whose latter years he soothed and sustained with so much devotion. That great Spirit now knows what he so often reflected on and pondered over.

The Queen deeply laments and mourns her noble Poet Laureate, who will be so universally regretted – but he has left undying works behind Him which we shall ever treasure.[1]

He was so very kind and full of sympathy to the Queen who alas! never saw him again after his last visit to Osborne.

Most deeply does the Queen feel for Lady Tennyson whose delicate health will, the Queen hopes, not suffer from this great shock. The blank will be terrible.

The Queen prays earnestly that they may all be sustained in this hour of grief and bereavement.

What was the cause of this fatal termination of his very short illness?

(Royal Archives, Windsor, R.44/2)

From Weimar   10.36 A.M.   *9th October,* 1892
To the Queen, Balmoral.   10.40 A.M.
Deeply deplore with you and the whole of Your Country the death of the Poet Laureate.

WILLIAM I.R. (Emperor of Germany)
(Royal Archives, Windsor, R.44/3A)

Balmoral.   *Oct.* 10*th,* 1892
4.7–4.16 P.M.
To: Mr Hallam Tennyson, Aldworth, Haslemere.

Anxious to know how your dear mother is. Think much of you all. You must be gratified at the universal feeling shown.

V.R.I.

From Haslemere.   6.58 P.M.   10*th October,* 1892
To the Queen, Balmoral.   7.12 P.M.
We are most grateful to Your Majesty. My Mother bears all as The Queen would wish her to do. We are deeply touched

---

[1] In a letter to Mr Gladstone the Queen wrote, 'A Tennyson we may not see again for a century, or – in all his originality – ever again –'. *The Queen & Mr Gladstone,* Philip Guedalla, vol. II p. 449 (Hodder & Stoughton, 1933).

by the Universal love and reverence shown to his memory.

HALLAM TENNYSON

(Royal Archives, Windsor, R.44/6)

From the Queen's diary.

Received a letter from Lord Tennyson of which I annex a copy.

13th October, 1892

Madam,

I have feared to intrude on your Majesty therefore I have not written until today in answer to the gracious inquiries respecting my Father's illness and thinking that the Queen might like to know also my impression of yesterday.

But first I must offer our most loyal and heartfelt thanks to Your Majesty for the beautiful wreaths and the Inscriptions.

My Father has never been quite the same since his bad illness four years ago.

Last February he caught a cold, and through the spring his cough harassed him greatly.

Latterly pain in his throat and jaw prevented him from taking much solid food – and for the last fortnight he could only swallow liquids.

The doctors attributed this to nervous exhaustion for they could discover no failure in any organ, and he could take walks of one and two miles about the moor here.

I think that your Majesty would care to know that the volume he asked for during the three latest days of his life was Shakespeare's *Cymbeline*. I said to him shortly before his passing away – 'You must not try and read it,' He answered, 'Let me feel it then,' and after a pause, 'I *have opened it*.' He kept it open at one of his favourite passages. –

> *Hang there like fruit, my soul,*
> *Till the tree dies.*

This must have been in answer to a message from my mother asking how he felt. He did not speak then – probably was too weak to say what he wished to say – and so opened the book.

On this his hand rested till he died. I could not part from this precious volume[1] – but we had a Shakespeare buried with

---

[1] This volume, the wreath of artificial laurel leaves sent by the Queen and many other relics of the funeral are now in the Tennyson Room at the Usher Art Gallery, Lincoln.

him – open at this passage which I marked. It was enclosed in a metal box.

We took him from our home by the light of the sunset and the stars in one of our carriages lined with moss and flowers and covered with a white pall woven by the Workwomen of the North at Keswick and embroidered with a wreath of the ancient poet's bay, wild roses, and the last stanza from his 'Crossing the Bar.' We did not venture to trouble your Majesty, but through Sir Dighton Probyn, the Prince of Wales gave us permission to cover my Father's coffin with the Flag of England. Your Majesty's Guards gave us one of theirs and it was buried with him.

The service today was most beautiful and impressive, simple and heart up lifting. Old Balaclava heroes, Gordon boys from the Gordon home at Woking, and English, Scottish, and Irish Volunteers lined the nave.

It may truly be said of the crowds of every rank present, as has been said, that each one seemed to be mourning for a friend.

The Queen will be glad to hear that my mother has borne all her sorrow with great heroism and that she feels with me that our life for the future is with him and for him, as it has striven to be in the past.

With our devoted and affectionate loyalty,

I am

Your Majesty's

Humble and devoted servant

HALLAM TENNYSON

(Royal Archives, Windsor, R.44/12)

Balmoral Castle

October 19th, 1892

I am much touched by your two kind letters and the copy of the beautiful lines which I conclude were the last He ever wrote! ['The Silent Voices'].

Everything must have been most Touching and beautiful and worthy of what the great Poet was – the 'passing away' with Shakespeare in his hand, the very simple and affecting departure from His own beloved Home, and the last sad ceremony when the mortal part of this great Man was laid in its final resting place.

I am thankful that your dear Mother is as well as could be
expected but the blank which for some time must only increase
will be terrible.

May I ask who Miss Mary Tennyson is – who has been
mentioned several times ?[1]

I am anxious to have a Bust of your dear Father at Windsor
and would like to know which is the best to have copied.

I found this short account of your Father's visit to me at
Osborne in 1883 which I had hastily written down in my
journal and have had it copied out – thinking it might perhaps
interest you.[2] Alas! I never saw him again. He was several
times ill and the weather prevented his moving so that I had
not the pleasure and comfort of again conversing with him
once more.

Hoping to see you when I return South,

believe me always
Yours truly,

Lord Tennyson   V.R.I.

POSTSCRIPT

Emily Lady Tennyson died on August 10th, 1896, in her
eighty-fourth year. Hallam informed the Queen in a letter, no
copy of which has been found.

Osborne,
August 13*th,* 1896

The Queen thanks Lord Tennyson for his kind letter and
wishes again to express to him her sincere sympathy with him
and Lady Tennyson in the loss of his dear Mother who was so
devoted a Wife to his Father. In the midst of their deep
affliction it must be a consolation to Lord Tennyson to feel
how he cheered and comforted the last years of both his dear
and revered Parents.

[1] The reference may be to Maud Tennyson, daughter of Horatio, Tennyson's
youngest brother, but 'Mary Tennyson' was the pseudonym of a novelist
whose real name was Mary H. Folkard. A list of her works will be found in
the Catalogue of the British Museum. She was writing between 1877 and
1897.

[2] See p. 102.

Aldworth,
Haslemere,
Surrey
August 16th, 1896

Madam,

I beg to offer my most grateful thanks for your Majesty's kind letter, and beautiful wreath, and also for allowing one of your gentlemen to represent you. Indeed your Majesty's letter was a comfort to me as far as any earthly comfort can go: and I took it to her grave with me.

The Queen's ever true and ready sympathy has ever been a help to us all, and I and mine can never forget it.

The sheaf was fully ripe to be garnered, but the sense of loss is none the less.

On Friday we sang, what we sang at my Father's funeral in the Abbey, 'Crossing the Bar', 'Silent Voices' (set to music by her) and Heber's hymn 'Holy, Holy.' Close to the home where she and my Father had passed so many happy years we rendered thanks to the Giver, for the beautiful, noble, holy and tender Spirit who is now with her beloved 'beyond the veil' having gained with him that Peace which passeth all understanding.

I am
Your Majesty's
ever most devoted and loyal servant
TENNYSON

Her last words were 'I have tried to be a good wife' – most touching – as if she were speaking to him.

(Lincoln, H.T.)

In the autumn of 1897 Hallam Lord Tennyson published his *Memoir* of his father, sending a copy to the Queen with the following letter.

Aldworth, Haslemere, Surrey *October 6th,* 1897
Madam,

May I venture to ask Your Majesty's acceptance of the accompanying *Memoir* of my Father, and to look first of all at my Father's dedication, which I pray you to accept as a kind of Jubilee Poem, written by one who was heart and soul devoted to his Queen. The great comfort that I have in my work is that it was a comfort to my Mother in her loneliness.

> I am
> with humble and loyal duty
> ever your Majesty's devoted servant,
> TENNYSON
> (Royal Archives, Windsor, F.40/94)

The dedication was as follows:

TO THE QUEEN

An unpublished version
of 'To the Queen', 1851

The noblest men methinks are bred
  Of ours the Saxo-Norman race;
  And in this world the noblest place,
Madam, is yours, our Queen and Head.

Your name is blown on every wind,
  Your flag thro' Austral ice is borne,
  And glimmers to the northern morn,
And floats in either Golden Ind.

I give this faulty book to you,
  For, tho' the faults be thick as dust
  In vacant chambers, I can trust
Your woman's nature kind and true.

> *Balmoral Castle*
> *October 9th,* 1897

The Queen has to thank Lord Tennyson for his kind letter as well as for the Copy of the Life of his father which she will read with much interest. She greatly admires the verses placed at the beginning which Lord Tennyson says were found amongst his unpublished pieces.

The Queen will ever retain a warm recollection of his Father's ever kind and ready sympathy evinced towards herself by her Poet Laureate, whose beautiful Poems she very greatly admires and which have immortalised his name.

> (Royal Archives, Windsor, F.40/95)

Hallam Tennyson's reply of October 14th, 1897, forms a fitting close to this story of a remarkable friendship.

Aldworth,
Haslemere,
Surrey

Madam,

With my whole heart I thank Your Majesty for writing me that beautiful letter with your own hand. If I may say so, few could understand my Father's sensitive and sympathetic nature like your Majesty who have yourself suffered and 'endured as seeing Him who is Invisible.'

I should like to add that the tributes to Your Majesty, that have reached me during these last few days, from all sorts and conditions of men, in consequence of those prefatory lines and of Your Majesty's own letters to my Father, have been very numerous and are overwhelmingly touching.

I am, Madam, with humble duty,
Your Majesty's ever grateful and loyal servant,
TENNYSON
(Royal Archives, Windsor, F.40/96)

APPENDIX

JUST over three years later on January 21st, 1901, the great Queen herself passed away. Hallam Tennyson, who was now Governor of South Australia, immediately telegraphed a message of sympathy to the Duke of Argyll, the Queen's son-in-law and son of his father's old friend, who had died in April the year before. The Duke's reply (oddly signed 'Lorne') of January 23rd shows how strongly the tradition of Tennyson's friendship was still maintained.

Kensington Palace, W.
Jan. 23, 1901

My dear Hallam – Very many thanks for so kindly telegraphing. We were both very glad to hear from you in this time of sorrow.

The afternoon of the 21st was a most disturbing time. The breathing seemed often so clogged, and the intimation was several times made by the Doctor that the death must come, and still it could not come, the strong heart still resisting the attack. My wife was on her knees for nearly 4 hours holding her mother's hand. The funeral will be the occasion of the show of much naval force, and the London route will be lined with troops. She has left very explicit directions. The sympathy shown wherever the English language is spoken is very touching.

Affectionate regards to Lady Tennyson from both of us.

Yours ever

LORNE

INDEX